CANADIAN
A–Z
OF GRAMMAR,
SPELLING, &
PUNCTUATION

Editor-in-ch ....naries
Katherine Barber

OXFORD
UNIVERSITY PRESS

OXFORD

UNIVERSITY PRESS

70 Wynford Drive, Don Mills, Ontario M3C 1J9
www.oup.com/ca

Oxford University Press is a department of the University of Oxford.
It furthers the University's objective of excellence in research, scholarship, and
education by publishing worldwide in

Oxford New York

Auckland Cape Town Dar es Salaam Hong Kong Karachi
Kuala Lumpur Madrid Melbourne Mexico City Nairobi
New Delhi Shanghai Taipei Toronto

With offices in

Argentina Austria Brazil Chile Czech Republic France Greece
Guatemala Hungary Italy Japan Poland Portugal Singapore South Korea
Switzerland Thailand Turkey Ukraine Vietnam

Oxford is a trade mark of Oxford University Press
in the UK and in certain other countries

Published in Canada by Oxford University Press

Library and Archives Canada Cataloguing in Publication

Canadian A to Z of grammar, spelling and punctuation /
edited by Katherine Barber and Robert Pontisso.

ISBN-10 : 0-19-542437-9

ISBN-13 : 978-0-19-542437-9

1. English language—Grammar—Dictionaries. 2. English
language—Usage—Dictionaries. 3. English language—Punctuation—
Dictionaries. I. Barber, Katherine, 1959– II. Pontisso, Robert, 1968-

PE1097.C35 2006   428'.003   C2005-906977-5

Cover design: Brett J. Miller

2 3 4 – 09 08 07

This book is printed on permanent (acid-free) paper ∞

Printed in Canada

CONTENTS

INTRODUCTION

The *Canadian A-Z of Grammar, Spelling, and Punctuation* is a handy problem-solver focusing on the difficulties that most people have with the English language. It is organized alphabetically so that you can find help for any problem as quickly and easily as possible, but it is not a comprehensive dictionary; for that you need to consult one of the range of Canadian Oxford dictionaries.

It provides grammar help so that you can avoid the most common grammatical errors, such as dangling participles, incorrect verb forms, and poor sentence structure. Definitions of grammatical terms like *phrase*, *clause*, and *conjunction* are identified by **G** in the margin.

The often-heard lament, "How can I look it up if I don't know how to spell it?" is symptomatic of the essential drawback of traditional alphabetically-organized spelling guides. While we have of course listed words in their proper alphabetical order, we have also included the most commonly misspelled words where people might *think* they belong, since that's where they're likely to be looked up. If you're unsure how to spell *pursue* (or indeed usually misspell it without realizing that you are doing so), the *per-* section might be the first place you'll check. In cases like this, we have noted the common misspelling with an ✗ beside it, followed by the correct spelling with a check mark, as in this stretch of entries:

fourth, forth
After *third* comes **fourth**. A formal word for *forward* is **forth**.

✗ fourty → forty ✔
Warning: there is no *u* in **forty**.

fowl, foul
A turkey is a type of **fowl**. Something unpleasant or unfair is **foul**.

The ⚠ icon in the margin identifies other words that are very commonly misspelled. To improve your spelling, you can focus on learning the correct spelling of these words.

But why look things up at all with the power of spell-checkers at your fingertips? Unfortunately, spell-checkers are not designed to alert you to the fact that you used *immanent* when you meant *imminent*, *levee* when you meant *levy*, or *silicon* when you meant *silicone*. Much of this guide consists of helpful descriptions of words that are often confused because they sound the same or are otherwise similar. You'll learn the distinction between *uninterested* and *disinterested*, the contrast between *imply* and *infer*, and the reason word historians get bugged when people mistake *entomology* for *etymology*.

To be helpful requires more than simply pointing out errors, and so we've also included lists of synonyms for commonplace words like *good*, *bad*, and *nice*, and we've included tips on tricky plural forms like *data*, *criteria*, *media*, and *phenomena*. At the end of the book you'll also find appendices providing guidance on the use of punctuation marks, listing irregular verb forms, and defining literary terms.

The information presented in this book is based on the extensive research conducted to produce the *Canadian Oxford Dictionary*.

abbreviation

G a word that is a shortened form of a longer word.

absolute

G **1** (of a construction) syntactically independent of the rest of the sentence, as in *dinner being over, we left the table*. **2** (of an adjective or transitive verb) used or usable without an expressed noun or object, e.g. *the hungry; guns kill*.

accelerate

⚠ Warning: **accelerate** starts with *ac-*, not *ex-*.

accept, except

When you receive something willingly you **accept** it. A word that means "not including" is **except**.

accessible

⚠ Warning: **accessible** ends in *-ible*, not *-able*.

accessory

⚠ Warning: **accessory** ends in *-ory*, not *-ary*.

accommodate

⚠ Warning: **accommodate** is spelled with two *c*'s and two *m*'s.

accordion

⚠ Warning: the ending of **accordion** is spelled *-ion*, not *-ian*.

✗ accross → across ✔

Warning: **across** is spelled with only one *c*.

acquaint, acquire, acquit

⚠ Warning: Don't forget the *c* in **acquaint**, **acquire**, and **acquit**.

acronym

G a word formed from the first letters of the words that make up the name of something, e.g. AIDS for "acquired immune deficiency syndrome". Use acronyms only when you are sure you know that your audience knows what the acronym means.

across

 Warning: Don't double the *c* in **across**.

active

G (also **active voice**) the form of a verb whose grammatical subject is the person or thing that performs the action, e.g. of the verbs in *guns kill; we saw him*. Often it is better to use the active voice when writing than the passive voice; *I sent the letter* is more effective than *The letter was sent by me*.

the actual facts

Phrases like **the actual facts** are redundant and should be avoided in writing. Simply say **the facts**.

ad, add

An advertisement is an **ad**. To combine numbers or things is to **add** them.

adapt, adept

To modify something for a purpose is to **adapt** it. Someone who is highly skilled or talented at something is **adept** at it.

adjective

G a word or phrase describing a person or thing, e.g. *big, red*, and *clever* in *a big house, red wine*, and *a clever idea*.

adjunct

G a word or phrase used to explain or amplify the predicate, subject, etc.: In *"She went home yesterday"* and *"He ran away in a panic"*, *"yesterday"* and *"in a panic"* are adjuncts.

A

adverb
G a word or phrase that modifies or qualifies another word (especially an adjective, verb, or other adverb) or a word group, expressing a relation of place, time, cause, degree, etc. (e.g. *gently, here, now, very*). Adverbs often answer the questions "how?", "how much?", "where?" and "when?". Some adverbs, called sentence adverbs, can also be used to modify whole sentences, e.g. *fortunately, they had a good dictionary*.

adverse, averse
Do not confuse **adverse** with **averse**. **Adverse** means "unfavourable" or "harmful", as in *Adverse weather conditions will make the move difficult*. **Averse** is used of people, nearly always with **to**, and means "having a strong dislike of or opposition to", as in *I am not averse to helping Vince move*.

advertise
⚠ Warning: **advertise** ends in *-ise*, not *-ize*.

advice, advise
A suggestion is **advice**. To offer a suggestion is to **advise**.

affect, effect
Affect is a verb that means "to have an influence on": *Alcohol affects drivers' concentration*. **Effect**, especially in the phrase *have an effect on*, is a noun that means "a result or influence": *Alcohol has a very bad effect on drivers*. **Effect** is also a formal verb meaning "to achieve": *People lack confidence in their ability to effect change in society*. Sometimes people confuse the verbs **affect** and **effect**.

affirmative
G stating that a fact is so; making an assertion: *affirmative sentences*.

 afficionado → aficionado ✔
Warning: there is only one *f* in **aficionado**.

afterward, afterword
The spelling is **afterwards** or **afterward** for "later on".
The concluding part of a book is the **afterword**.

aggravate
The use of **aggravate** to mean "annoy" is well
established, despite being considered incorrect by some.

aggressive
 Warning: **aggressive** is spelled with two *g*'s and two *s*'s.

ago
The correct construction is *It was ten years **ago that** I moved
to Vancouver*, not *It is ten years ago since I moved to Vancouver*.

ain't
Ain't is unacceptable in spoken and written English
except in intentionally humorous and very informal
contexts and phrases, such as *You **ain't** seen nothing yet!*

air, err
What we breathe is **air**. To make a mistake is to **err**.

ale, ail
To suffer or be sick is to **ail**. A type of beer is **ale**.

Algonquin, Algonquian
The word **Algonquin** refers to an Aboriginal people
living around the Ottawa River. The word **Algonquian**
refers to a wider group of Aboriginal peoples speaking
related languages, including the **Algonquin**, the
Blackfoot, the Cree, the Mi'kmaq, the Ojibwa, and others.
The use of **Algonquin** to refer to the **Algonquian**
peoples or language group is incorrect.

all (of)
All of the following are correct: ***all of** the bread, **all** the
bread; **all of** our members, **all** our members*.

A

alley, ally
A lane is an **alley** (plural **alleys**). A partner is an **ally** (plural **allies**).

all-points bulletin
The term **all-points bulletin** is not used by police forces in Canada, who use **general alert** instead.

allot, a lot
To give or apportion something to someone is to **allot** it. A large amount is **a lot**.

allusion, illusion
When you make an indirect or passing reference to something you are making an **allusion**. A false impression or a picture that deceives one's eyes is an **illusion**.

ally, alley
A partner is an **ally** (plural **allies**). A lane is an **alley** (plural **alleys**).

a lot
 Warning: **a lot** is not spelled as a single word.

already, all ready
Do not confuse **already** with **all ready**. **Already** means "beforehand", as in I have **already** brushed my teeth. **All ready** means "entirely ready", as in I have brushed my teeth and now I am **all ready** for bed.

alright, all right
Although **alright** is quite common in informal writing, many people still object to it. To be safe you should always spell it as two words: **all right**.

altar, alter
A table at the front of a church is an **altar**. When you change something you **alter** it.

altogether, all together

Altogether does not mean the same as **all together**.
Altogether means "in total", as in *If Paul comes there will
be six of us **altogether***, or "in all respects, totally", as in
*The novel is **altogether** too complex*, whereas **all together**
means "all at once" or "all in one place", as in *Paul and
his friends were **all together** at the show.*

amend

 Warning: there is only one *m* in **amend**.

among, between

Some people argue that **between** should be used only to
express a relationship involving two people or things and
among should be used when more than two are involved. In
fact, the use of **between** in situations involving more than
two is well established and acceptable, as in *We divided the
profits **between** the four of us* or ***Between** playing softball,
coaching soccer, and reffing hockey, Diego hardly has time to study.*

amphitheatre

Warning: **amphitheatre** is spelled with an *h*
immediately following the *p*: ***amphi-***.

ancestor, descendant

Do not confuse **ancestor** and **descendant**. Your
ancestors are your parents, grandparents, great-
grandparents, etc. Your **descendants** are your children,
grandchildren, great-grandchildren, etc.

angel, angle

A heavenly being is an **angel**. A corner or slant is an
angle; **angle** also means "to catch fish".

anoint

 Warning: When you apply oil to a person's head as part of a
religious rite you **anoint** them. Do not double the *n* in **anoint**.

anomaly
⚠ Warning: the ending of **anomaly** is *-aly*, not *-oly*.

ante, anti
The spelling is **ante** in *up the **ante***. The spelling is **anti** for the meaning "opposed to".

antecedent
G a word, phrase, clause, or sentence, to which a following word (especially a pronoun, usually following) refers: in *He grabbed the ball and threw it in the air*, *ball* is the antecedent of *it*.

antonym
G a word opposite in meaning to another, e.g. *bad* and *good*. Compare SYNONYM.

anxious
The use of **anxious** to mean "eager", as in *I'm **anxious** to meet Marie-Claire*, is well established, despite being considered incorrect by some.

anymore, any more
Always spell **any more** as two words when specifying a quantity of something, as in *Surely, Tony, you can't eat **any more** ice cream!* Spell it as one word when you mean "any longer", as in *I don't like this **anymore**!*

anyone, any one
Note the difference between **anyone** and **any one**: *Conrad won't talk to **anyone**; **any one** of us could have upset him.*

apartment
⚠ Warning: **apartment** is spelled with only one *p*.

apology
⚠ Warning: there is only one *p* in **apology**.

apostrophe
For guidance on the use of the apostrophe see Appendix 1.

apposition
G the placing of a word next to another, especially the addition of one noun to another, in order to qualify or explain the first, e.g. *William the Conqueror; my friend Sue.*

 aquaint, aquire, aquit → **acquaint, acquire, acquit** ✔
Warning: **acquaint**, **acquire**, and **acquit** are spelled with a *c*.

arc, ark
A curve is an **arc**; **arc** is also the spelling in ***arc** lamp*. The spelling is **ark** in *Noah's **ark**, Holy **Ark**,* and ***Ark** of the Covenant.*

arctic
Some people claim that it is lazy to pronounce ***arctic*** as "AR tick", but in fact this is the original English pronunciation of the word, which was spelled with only the final *c* from its introduction in the 1400s until it was rewritten with two *c*'s in imitation of Latin in the 1600s. Either pronunciation is correct.

arctic, Arctic
⚠ Warning: do not forget the *c* before the *t* in **arctic**. Spell **Arctic** with a capital *A* when referring to the northern region: *They spent four years in the **Arctic***, but with a lower case *a* when referring simply to cold conditions: *Everyone must bring an **arctic** sleeping bag.*

ark, arc
The spelling is **ark** in *Noah's **ark**, Holy **Ark**,* and ***Ark** of the Covenant.* A curve is an **arc**; **arc** is also the spelling in ***arc** lamp*.

arm's-length, arm's length
Note the difference in spelling between *an **arm's-length** relationship* and *the refugee board operates at **arm's length** from the government*. There is no hyphen when the latter kind of structure is used.

✗ **artic, Artic** → **arctic, Arctic** ✔
Warning: do not forget the *c* before the *t* in **arctic**.

article
G any of the words *the* (the definite article), *a*, or *an* (the indefinite articles).

ascent, assent
A rise is an **ascent**. A word for "consent" or "agreement" is **assent**; to agree is to **assent**.

asphalt
⚠ Warning: there is no *h* before the *p* in **asphalt**.

assent, ascent
A word for "consent" or "agreement" is **assent**; to agree is to **assent**. A rise is an **ascent**.

attributive
G (of adjectives or nouns) used before a noun to describe it; in *the blue sky* and *a family business, blue* and *family* are attributive. Compare PREDICATIVE.

auger, augur
A tool for boring a hole or clearing a drain is an **auger**. When something acts as a sign that things will go well it is said to **augur** well.

auxiliary verb
G a verb used in forming tenses, moods, and voices of other verbs, e.g. *will* in *She will go*.

averse, adverse
Do not confuse **averse** with **adverse**. **Averse** is used of
people, nearly always with **to**, and means "having a strong
dislike of or opposition to", as in *I am not **averse to** helping
Vince move*. **Adverse** means "unfavourable" or "harmful", as
in ***Adverse** weather conditions will make the move difficult*.

avocado
 Warning: **avocado** begins *avo-*, not *ava-*.

aware (of)
The use of **aware** in sentences like *The recycling program has
been successful because people today are so **aware*** is ambiguous
and not well established. It is better to say *The recycling
program has been successful because people today are very **aware**
of environmental issues* or *The recycling program has been
successful because people today are very environmentally **aware***.

Axel, axil, axle
The figure skating jump is an **Axel**; part of a plant is an
axil; wheels are attached to an **axle**.

bachelor
 Warning: there is no *t* in **bachelor**.

bad, very bad
Instead of saying that something is **bad** or **very bad**, try to
use more precise and interesting adjectives to describe things:

> *her handwriting is **poor**/**atrocious**/**appalling**/**illegible***
> *a **foul**/**disgusting**/**putrid**/**fetid** odour*
> *the villain is **evil**/**wicked**/**dishonest**/**corrupt***
> *a **serious**/**severe**/**dreadful** injury*
> ***awful**/**terrible**/**inclement**/**nasty** weather*
> *an **unfortunate**/an **upsetting**/a **traumatic** experience*
> *a **naughty**/**disobedient**/**mischievous**/**unruly** child*
> *an **awkward**/**embarrassing**/**unmanageable***
>   *situation*

the meal was **poor/unsatisfactory/unacceptable/
   unpalatable**
his eyesight is **poor/weak**
the bus service on Don Mills is **execrable/ludicrously
   inadequate**

To refer to your health, you can say: *I feel* **unwell/sick/
terrible**, or: *I don't feel* **(very) well**.
Instead of saying: *She feels* **bad** *about what she did*, you
can say: *She feels* **guilty/regretful/remorseful/
apologetic**.

bail, bale
Money paid for the temporary release of a prisoner is
bail; **bail** is also the spelling for **bail** *out*. A bundle of
hay is a **bale**.

baited, bated
A hook with bait is **baited**. To wait anxiously is to wait
with **bated** breath.

bale, bail
A bundle of hay is a **bale**. Money paid for the temporary
release of a prisoner is **bail**; **bail** is also the spelling for
bail *out*.

ball, bawl
A spherical toy, a grand dance, or a good time is a **ball**.
To weep loudly is to **bawl**; to scold someone severely is
to **bawl** them **out**.

bare bones, bare-bones
Note the difference in spelling between the structures *the*
bare bones *of the plot* and *a* **bare-bones** *budget of
$100,000*.

bare, bear
Something that is uncovered is **bare**; **bare** also means
"the least amount necessary" in phrases like *the* **bare**

essentials; to reveal or uncover something is to **bare** it. The animal is spelled **bear**; **bear** is also the spelling for "bring", "endure", and "give birth to".

baron, barren

A nobleman or powerful business person is a **baron**. Land that is unable to produce plants is **barren**.

base, bass

The spelling is **base** for "foundation", "headquarters", "low", and "establish". A voice or instrument with a low pitch is a **bass**.

✗ batchelor → bachelor ✔

Warning: there is no *t* in **bachelor**.

bated, baited

To wait anxiously is to wait with **bated** breath. A hook with bait is **baited**.

bawl, ball

To weep loudly is to **bawl**; to scold someone severely is to **bawl** them **out**. A spherical toy, a grand dance, or a good time is a **ball**.

bazaar, bizarre

A large market or store is a **bazaar**. Something very strange is **bizarre**.

beach, beech

The sandy shore is a **beach**. The tree is a **beech**.

bear, bare

The animal is spelled **bear**; **bear** is also the spelling for "bring", "endure", and "give birth to". Something that is uncovered is **bare**; **bare** also means "the least amount necessary" in phrases like *the **bare** essentials*; to reveal or uncover something is to **bare** it.

B

bear, borne, born

Borne is the standard past participle of the verb **bear**, e.g. *Sara has **borne** a son, The children were **borne** on his shoulders,* or *Youssef has never **borne** a grudge.* **Born** is used only in reference to birth, as in *Megan was **born** in February* or *Jason was **born** lucky.*

beat, beaten

Note that the past participle of **beat** is **beaten**: *We were **beaten** by a better team.*

beat, beet

To strike or defeat is to **beat**; a rhythm is a **beat**. The vegetable is a **beet**.

beech, beach

The tree is a **beech**. The sandy shore is a **beach**.

beet, beat

The vegetable is a **beet**. To strike or defeat is to **beat**; a rhythm is a **beat**.

beg the question

The expression **beg the question** can be used to mean "raise the issue" or "invite the obvious question", as in *The rising cost of gasoline prices **begs the question**, how long can we afford to keep driving our cars?* This is by far the most common use today and widely accepted, despite the fact that some people feel **beg the question** should only be used in its original sense, "assume the truth of an argument without arguing it", as in *By spending so much on education in the fight against drugs, we are **begging the question** of the effectiveness of education,* i.e. we are assuming that through education we can radically reduce drug-taking.

bellow, below

To shout is to **bellow**. Another word for "underneath" is **below**.

B

berry, bury
A small juicy fruit is a **berry**. To place something under dirt is to **bury** it.

berserk
⚠ Warning: Don't forget the first *r* in **berserk**.

besiege
⚠ Warning: the *i* comes before the second *e*.

better, bettor
Better means "more excellent". A person who bets is a **bettor**.

between, among
Some people argue that **between** should be used only to express relationship involving two people or things and **among** should be used when more than two are involved. In fact, the use of **between** in situations involving more than two is well established and acceptable, as in *We divided the profits **between** the four of us* or ***Between** playing softball, coaching soccer, and reffing hockey, Diego hardly has time to study.*

between you and me
In standard English it is correct to say **between you and me** but incorrect to say "between you and I".

biannual, biennial
Do not confuse **biannual** with **biennial**. **Biannual** means "occurring two times each year". **Biennial** means "occurring one time every two years".

bicep, biceps
Although **bicep** is becoming more common, it is still considered informal. **Biceps** remains the standard form for both the singular noun and its plural.

biennial, biannual
Do not confuse **biennial** with **biannual**. **Biennial** means "occurring one time every two years". **Biannual** means "occurring two times each year".

bimonthly
The word **bimonthly** is ambiguous, since it can mean either "two times every month" or "one time every two months". Use alternatives like **twice monthly** and **semi-monthly** for the first meaning or **every two months** for the second.

birth, berth
A child emerges from its mother at **birth**. **Berth** is the spelling in *playoff* **berth**; a **berth** is also a bunk on a ship or train.

bite, byte
To tear or puncture with the teeth is to **bite**. The computing term is **byte**.

biweekly
The word **biweekly** is ambiguous, since it can mean either "two times every week" or "one time every two weeks". Use alternatives like **twice weekly** and **semi-weekly** for the first meaning or **every two weeks** for the second.

bizarre, bazaar
Something very strange is **bizarre**. A large market or store is a **bazaar**.

block, bloc
A cubic or rectangular solid is a **block**; an obstruction is a **block**. An alliance of people or nations is a **bloc**: *Bloc Québécois*; *the Eastern* **bloc**.

blond, blonde
The form **blonde** is more likely to be used of females than of males, e.g. *Rachel's hair is **blonde** today*. **Blond** can be used of both males and females, e.g. *Eugene and Isadora make an attractive couple because they're both **blonds***.

boar, bore
The wild pig is a **boar**. Something dull is a **bore**; **bore** is also the spelling for ***bore** a hole*, *tidal **bore***, and *12-**bore** shotgun*.

boarder, border
Someone who boards or lives at another's house is a **boarder**. A pattern around the edge of something or the division between two territories is a **border**.

bobble, bauble
To fumble is to **bobble**; a small tufted ball of wool is a **bobble**. A small ornament or piece of jewellery is a **bauble**.

bod, baud
An informal term for "body" is **bod**. The computing term is **baud**.

bonus
The phrase **added bonus**, as in *They threw in a key chain as an added bonus*, is redundant and should be avoided in writing. It is better to say *They threw in a key chain as a **bonus***.

bookkeeper, bookkeeping
Remember to double the *k* in **bookkeeper** and **bookkeeping**.

border, boarder
A pattern around the edge of something or the division between two territories is a **border**. Someone who boards or lives at another's house is a **boarder**.

bore, boar
Something dull is a **bore**; **bore** is also the spelling for *bore a hole, tidal bore,* and *12-bore shotgun*. The wild pig is a **boar**.

born, borne
Born is used only in reference to birth, as in *Megan was born in February* or *Jason was born lucky*. The standard past participle used with all senses of the verb **bear** is **borne**, as in *Sara has borne a son, The children were borne on his shoulders,* or *Youssef has never borne a grudge*.

bouillon, bullion
Broth is **bouillon**. Gold or silver in blocks is **bullion**.

boy, buoy
A young male is a **boy**. An anchored float is a **buoy**.

brackets
For guidance on the use of brackets see Appendix 1.

brake, break
A device that stops a car is a **brake**. A pause is a **break**; to shatter is to **break**.

breach, breech, breeches
The breaking of a contract is a **breach**. The part of a gun is a **breech**; short trousers are **breeches**; **breech** is also the spelling in *breech birth*.

break, brake
To shatter is to **break**. A device that stops a car is a **brake**; a pause is a break.

breath, breathe
Air inhaled or exhaled is **breath**. To inhale and exhale is to **breathe**.

breech, breach

The part of a gun is a **breech**; short trousers are
breeches; **breech** is also the spelling in *breech* birth.
The breaking of a contract is a **breach**.

bridal, bridle

The spelling is **bridal** if you are referring to brides and
weddings. A horse's headgear is a **bridle**; if you get upset
and resentful about something, you **bridle**; **bridle** is also
the spelling in *bridle* path.

broach, brooch

When you raise a subject for discussion you **broach** it.
The piece of jewellery is a **brooch**.

broccoli

⚠ Warning: **broccoli** is spelled with two *c*'s and one *l*.

bullion, bouillon

Gold or silver in bulk is **bullion**. A type of broth is
bouillon.

bury, berry

To place something under dirt is to **bury** it. A small juicy
fruit is a **berry**.

business, busyness

A person's job or company is their **business**. A state of
being busy is **busyness**: *He has been very busy, and he
expects his busyness to continue.*

Caesar

⚠ Warning: **Caesar** is spelled with *ae*.

calendar, calender

A chart showing the days, weeks, and months of a year is
a **calendar**. A machine for pressing cloth or paper is a
calender.

callous, callus
An insensitive person is **callous**. The usual Canadian spelling for an area of hard skin is **callus**.

cannon, canon
A large gun is a **cannon** (plural **cannon** or **cannons**). A general rule, a list of works, or a musical composition is a **canon**.

canvas, canvass
A kind of cloth is **canvas**. To ask people for donations or for opinions is to **canvass**.

capital, Capitol
The spelling is **capital** for a main city, an upper case letter, money, the top part of a pillar, and in *capital punishment*. The US legislative building is the **Capitol**.

capital letters
For guidance on the use of capital letters see Appendix 1.

carat, karat
Diamonds are measured in **carats**. The purity of gold is measured in **karats**.

could/couldn't care less
Using **could care less** instead of the more logical **couldn't care less** is perceived by many people as a sign of sloppiness or total disregard for the language. Both of these expressions are informal, so if you are writing or making a formal speech, you would be better off using something else altogether, such as *I am totally indifferent.*

carol, carrel
A song is a **carol**. A desk or cubicle in a library is a **carrel**.

carrot, karat, carat
The root vegetable is a **carrot**. The purity of gold is

measured in **karats**. Diamonds are measured in **carats**.

cash, cache
Money is **cash**. A hiding place or a small supply is a **cache**.

cashmere, Kashmir
The spelling is **cashmere** for the soft wool. A region of South Asia is **Kashmir**.

✗ Ceasar → **Caesar** ✔
Warning: **Caesar** is spelled with *ae*.

cement, concrete
The use of **cement** to mean **concrete** rather than the binding substance in concrete has been criticized, but in non-technical contexts, such uses as *cement floor* or *cement sidewalk* are unambiguous.

censer, censor, censure, sensor
A vessel for burning incense is a **censer**. To remove something objectionable from a book or movie is to **censor** it; a person who removes such matter is a **censor**. To criticize something harshly is to **censure** it. A device that detects light or motion is a **sensor**.

cereal, serial
Grain or breakfast food is **cereal**. Something produced in series or in instalments is **serial**; **serial** is also the spelling in *serial killer*.

chalk, chock
The stick for writing on blackboards is a **chalk**. A wooden block is a **chock**; **chock** is also the spelling in *chock full*.

changeover, change over
The verb is spelled **change over**: *Our store is going to change over from plastic bags to paper*. The noun is spelled

changeover: *There was much confusion during the changeover*.

cheap, cheep
Something inexpensive or unworthy is **cheap**. The cry of a bird is a **cheep**.

check, cheque
The spelling is **check** for "examine" and "stop" and in *check* mark and *bodycheck*; a restaurant bill is a **check**. **Cheque** is the usual Canadian spelling for the method of payment: *cash a **cheque**; deposit a **paycheque***.

check in, check-in
The verb is spelled **check in**: *Watch the bags and I'll go check in*. The noun is spelled **check-in**: *The guy at the check-in told us to wait outside*.

checkout, check out
The verb is spelled **check out**: *I waited in the lobby while she went to check out*. The noun is spelled **checkout**: *Take all parcels to the checkout*.

check up, checkup
The verb is spelled **check up**: *We'd better check up on his story*. The noun is spelled **checkup**: *Your next checkup is in six months*.

cheep, cheap
The cry of a bird is a **cheep**. Something inexpensive or unworthy is **cheap**.

Chile, chili, chilly
The country in South America is **Chile**. The pepper or the spicy food is **chili**. Something cold is **chilly**.

Chipewyan, Chippewa
Do not confuse the **Chipewyans** and the **Chippewa**.

The **Chipewyans** are an Athapaskan people living in northwestern Canada. The **Chippewa** are the Ojibwa living south and west of the Great Lakes.

C

chock, chalk
A wooden block is a **chock**; **chock** is also the spelling in *chock full*. The stick for writing on blackboards is a **chalk**.

choral, coral, chorale, corral
Music sung by a choir is **choral** music. The substance found in the sea is **coral**. A **chorale** is a type of hymn tune. A **corral** is a pen for horses.

chord, cord
The spelling is **chord** for notes sounded together, for a line joining two points of a circle, and in *to touch a chord*. The spelling is **cord** for a rope and in *spinal **cord*** and *vocal **cords***.

chow, ciao
The spelling is **chow** for the food and the dog. The Italian greeting is **ciao**.

City Hall, city hall
The word **city hall** is often spelled with capital letters when it is used as the name for a specific **city hall**: *We're staying in a hotel across the street from **City Hall**.*

clamp down, clampdown
The verb is spelled **clamp down**: *Police have started to clamp down on crime.* The noun is spelled **clampdown**: *Resistance groups have been nervous since the government clampdown on street protests.*

clause
G a group of words that consists of a subject and verb, and which may constitute a sentence or part of a sentence. In the sentence *They often go to Italy because they love the food,*

They often go to Italy is the main or PRINCIPAL CLAUSE, and *because they love the food* is the SUBORDINATE CLAUSE.

claw back, clawback
The verb is spelled **claw back**: *The government intends to **claw back** $25M by increasing property taxes.* The noun is spelled **clawback**: *There's growing anger at the pension **clawback**.*

climatic, climactic
Do not confuse **climatic** with **climactic**. **Climatic** means "having to do with the weather or climate", as in *Dinosaurs may have become extinct as a result of **climatic** changes*. **Climactic** means "happening at the most exciting or important moment", as in *The movie ends when the criminals are finally caught in a **climactic** car chase*.

climb, clime
To ascend is to **climb**. A region considered in terms of its weather is a **clime**.

coarse, course
Something that is rough is **coarse**. A track, a series of classes, or a part of a meal is a **course**.

coliseum, Colosseum
A large theatre or stadium is a **coliseum**. The large ancient amphitheatre in Rome is the **Colosseum**.

collective noun
G a grammatically singular noun that denotes a collection or number of individuals, e.g. *assembly, family, troop*.

colon
For guidance on the use of the colon see Appendix 1.

coma, comma
A state of unconsciousness is a **coma**. The punctuation mark is a **comma**.

comma

For guidance on the use of the comma see Appendix 1.

C

comma splice

G a faulty construction where two independent clauses are joined without a conjunction, with a comma between them, or when a subordinate clause introduced by a conjunctive adverb is introduced by a comma rather than a semi-colon. *I really enjoyed my holiday, I love to travel* and *I would love to go back there, however I can't afford it* are both examples of comma splices. Both can be corrected by replacing the comma with a semicolon.

committee

⚠ Warning: **committee** is spelled with two *m*'s, two *t*'s, and two *e*'s.

common noun

G (also **common name**) a name denoting a class of objects or a concept as opposed to a particular individual, e.g. *boy*, *beauty*.

comparative

G (of an adjective or adverb) expressing a higher degree of a quality, but not the highest possible, e.g. *braver*, *more fiercely*. When singling out which of two items is better, larger, etc., use the comparative form. Say it is *the better of the two*, not *the best of the two*.

complement

G a word or phrase, especially an adjective or a noun, that is used after linking verbs such as *be* and *become*, e.g. *angry* in *He became angry*.

complement, compliment

Something added to enhance or improve something else is a **complement**: *A burgundy necktie may **complement** a* *blue suit.* When you praise someone, you **compliment** them or pay a **compliment**.

complementary, complimentary

Someone who praises you or something given free of charge is **complimentary**. An accessory that enhances or improves an outfit is **complementary**.

comprise

Such uses as *The team **is comprised of** six players* and *Women **comprise** a large proportion of the class* are strongly opposed by some, who prefer *The team is composed* (or *made up*) *of six players* and *Women constitute* (or *make up*) *a large proportion of the class*. The disputed uses are very common, however, and considered acceptable by many.

comrade, camaraderie

An associate or friend is a **comrade**. Friendship among associates is **camaraderie**.

concede

⚠ Warning: **concede** ends in *-ede*, not *-eed*.

✗ concensus → consensus ✔

Warning: the word **consensus** does not include the word *census*.

concession

⚠ Warning: in **concession** the *n* is followed by a *c*, not an *s*.

confidant, confidante, confident

A friend you tell secrets to is a **confidant**. A female friend you tell secrets to is a **confidante**. Someone who is self-assured is **confident**.

conditional

G a clause or sentence that expresses a condition on which

something depends, e.g. the first clause in *If she wins, we will be rich*.

C

conjugation
G the variation of the form of a verb to show its voice, mood, tense, number, and person.

conjunction
G a word used to connect clauses or sentences or words in the same clause, e.g. *and, but, if, because*. There are COORDINATING CONJUNCTIONS, CORRELATIVE CONJUNCTIONS, and SUBORDINATING CONJUNCTIONS.

conjunctive adverb
G an adverb that joins whole clauses to each other and indicates the nature of the connection. Common conjunctive adverbs are: *accordingly, afterward(s), also, anyway, besides, certainly, consequently, conversely, finally, further, furthermore, hence, however, indeed, instead, interestingly, later, likewise, meanwhile, moreover, namely, nevertheless, next, nonetheless, otherwise, similarly, still, subsequently, then, thereafter, therefore, thus, undoubtedly*. It is **very important** to use a semi-colon and not just a comma between clauses joined with a conjunctive adverb, and to put a comma after the conjunctive adverb: *It was late and she was tired; however, her essay was due the next morning, so she continued working.*

consensus
⚠ Warning: the word **consensus** does not include the word *census*.

✗ consession → concession ✔
Warning: in **concession** the *n* is followed by a *c*, not an *s*.

continual, continuous
Note the difference between **continual** and

continuous: **continual** refers to something happening frequently, with intervals, as in *I couldn't work because of the **continual** interruptions*; **continuous** refers to something that is non-stop, as in *I couldn't sleep because of the **continuous** pounding of rain on the roof*. Only **continuous** can refer to something uninterrupted over a distance, as in *a **continuous** row of houses* or *a **continuous** stretch of road*.

coo, coup
The sound of a dove is a **coo**. A sudden overthrow of government or a successful event is a **coup**.

coop, coupe
A pen for chickens is a **coop**. A kind of car is a **coupe**.

coordinating conjunction
G any of a number of conjunctions (*and, or, but, nor, yet, for, so, whereas*) which can join independent clauses. Use a comma before the conjunction separating independent clauses, e.g. *I wanted to go to the ballet, but I couldn't afford it*.

copyright, copywriter
The legal right to publish or perform material is **copyright**. A person who writes text for ads is a **copywriter**.

coral, choral, chorale, corral
The substance found in the sea is **coral**. Music sung by a choir is **choral** music. A **chorale** is a type of hymn tune. A **corral** is a pen for horses.

cord, chord
The spelling is **cord** for a rope and in *spinal **cord*** and *vocal **cords***. The spelling is **chord** for notes sounded together, for a line joining two points of a circle, and in *to touch a **chord***.

core, corps
The central part of something is the **core**. A group of people is a **corps**: *army* **corps**; *press* **corps**; *dancers in the* **corps**.

cornet, coronet
A musical instrument like a trumpet is a **cornet**. A small crown is a **coronet**.

corps, corpse
A group of people is a **corps**: *army* **corps**; *press* **corps**; *dancers in the* **corps**. A dead body is a **corpse**.

corpulent
Corpulent is considered a more formal and somewhat more polite and less blunt synonym for *fat* or *obese*: *I could visualize him growing moustachioed,* **corpulent**, *with a gold pocket watch in his vest.*

corral, choral, coral, chorale
A **corral** is a pen for horses. Music sung by a choir is **choral** music. The substance found in the sea is **coral**. A **chorale** is a type of hymn tune.

correlative conjunctions
G the conjunctions corresponding to each other and regularly used together: *neither* and *nor*, *either* and *or* are correlative conjunctions.

could have
Note that in statements such as *You* **could have** *tried harder*, the correct expression is **could have** (or the informal contraction **could've**) and not *could of*.

coulee, coulis
A deep ravine is a **coulee**. A fruit purée is a **coulis**.

council, counsel
A group of people elected to manage affairs is a **council**.

When you advise a person, you **counsel** them; a lawyer is a **counsel**.

councillor, counsellor
A member of a council is a **councillor**. An adviser or a supervisor is a **counsellor**.

counsel, council
When you advise a person, you **counsel** them; a lawyer is a **counsel**. A group of people elected to manage affairs is a **council**.

counsellor, councillor
An adviser or a supervisor is a **counsellor**. A member of a council is a **councillor**.

countable noun
a noun that can form a plural or be used with the indefinite article, e.g. *car*, *book*, *child*.

coup, coupe
A sudden overthrow of government or a successful event is a **coup**. A kind of car is a **coupe**.

a couple (of)
The use of **couple** without **of**, as in *I had a **couple** beers*, is highly informal and should be avoided in writing.

course, coarse
A track, a series of classes, or a part of a meal is a **course**. Something that is rough is **coarse**.

creak, creek
A harsh scraping or squeaking sound is a **creak**. A stream or brook is a **creek**.

credible, creditable
Do not confuse **credible** with **creditable**. **Credible**

means "believable", as in *The lawyers tried to show that the witness was not **credible***. **Creditable** means "worthy of praise but not outstanding", as in *Jenny and Clive turned in a **creditable** performance in the three-legged race, finishing fifth*.

creek, creak
A stream or brook is a **creek**. A harsh scraping or squeaking sound is a **creak**.

criterion, criteria
Criteria is a plural noun: *Eligibility **criteria** have been tightened*. It should not be used as a singular. The singular of **criteria** is **criterion**: *Hard work was the **criterion** by which people were judged in the West*.

cue, queue
A signal or a rod used in billiards is a **cue**. A lineup or a sequence of computer tasks is a **queue**.

currant, current
The fruit is a **currant**. The spelling is **current** for a stream or trend, and in ***current** events*.

cygnet, signet
A young swan is a **cygnet**. A small seal set in a ring is a **signet**.

cymbal, symbol
The musical instrument is a **cymbal**. A design representing something is a **symbol**.

dam, damn
A **dam** holds back water. To **damn** is to doom to hell; **damn** is also used as an interjection.

Dane, deign
A person from Denmark is a **Dane**. The spelling is **deign** in *Millicent would never **deign** to take the bus*.

dangling participles

A participle is a word formed as an inflection of the verb, such as *arriving* or *arrived*. A dangling participle is one which is left "hanging" because, in the grammar of the clause, it does not relate to the noun it should. In the sentence ***Arriving** at the airport, **she** picked up her bags* the construction is correct because the participle **arriving** and the subject **she** relate to each other (**she** is the one doing the **arriving**). But in the following sentence, a dangling participle has been created: ***Arriving** at the airport, **her bag** was missing.* We know, logically, that it is not **her bag** which was **arriving** but grammatically that is exactly the link that has been created. This sentence would have to be rewritten as *arriving at the airport, she found that her bag was missing.* Do not use dangling participles; they can cause real confusion.

dash

For guidance on the use of the dash see Appendix 1.

data, datum

In specialized scientific fields, **data** is treated as the plural of **datum**, taking a plural verb, as in *The **data** were collected and classified.* However, in modern non-scientific use, it is often treated similarly to a word like *information*, which takes a singular verb. Sentences like *The **data** was collected over a number of years* are now widely accepted in standard English.

dear, deer

Something cherished or expensive is **dear**. The animal is a **deer** (plural **deer**).

decease, disease

Death is **decease**. An illness is a **disease**.

decent, descent

Something acceptable or proper is **decent**. A downward movement or slope is a **descent**.

decimate

Historically, the meaning of **decimate** is "kill one in every ten". Although this sense has been almost completely superseded by the more general sense, "kill or destroy a large proportion of", it is important to recognize that a sentence like *The epidemic **decimated** the tiny town of 400 people* could be interpreted to mean that only ten percent of the town's residents died rather than a much greater number. For this reason, it may be better to use a word like **devastate**, **annihilate**, **obliterate**, or **destroy**.

declarative sentence

G a sentence that takes the form of a simple statement.

deductible

Note that **deductible** ends in *-ible*, not *-able*.

deer, dear

The animal is a **deer** (plural **deer**). Something cherished or expensive is **dear**.

defining clause

G (also **restrictive clause**) a clause specifying which particular thing or things are being discussed, as opposed to merely describing them; in *The books which are on the table used to belong to Anna*, the clause *which are on the table* is a defining clause because it tells us *which* books out of all the books in the world are the ones that used to belong to Anna. If, on the other had, you insert commas around the clause, *The books, which are on the table, used to belong to Anna*, it merely tells us where the books are and is therefore not defining. In a defining clause, *which* can be replaced by *that*: *The books that are on the table used to belong to Anna*.

definite, definitive

Definite should not be used as a synonym for **definitive**. **Definite** means clear, unambiguous, and without doubt, as in *The demonstrators were making a* ***definite*** *statement of their concerns about the prime minister's economic policy*. **Definitive** means authoritative, unconditional, and final, as in *The prime minister issued a* ***definitive*** *statement outlining her economic policy*.

D

definite article

G the word (*the* in English) preceding a noun and implying a specific or known instance e.g. *the book on the table*.

defuse, diffuse

You can **defuse** a bomb or a tense situation. To spread or disperse is to **diffuse**: *The sunlight was* ***diffused*** *by the thin clouds*; something spread out is **diffuse**.

degree

G any of three stages (positive, comparative, superlative) in the comparison of an adjective or adverb.

demonstrative

G (of an adjective or pronoun) indicating the person or thing referred to, e.g. *this, that, these, those*.

dependant, dependent

A person who relies on another is a **dependant**. The usual Canadian spelling for "determined by" or "unable to do without" is **dependent**: *Caspar is* ***dependent*** *upon his uncle*.

dependent clause

G (also **subordinate clause**) a clause, usually introduced by a conjunction, that does not constitute a sentence itself but which depends on the principal clause that it modifies or in which it serves as a noun, e.g. *that she has come* in *I hope that she has come* or *because I was angry* in *I shouted because I was angry*. A dependent clause used on its own without a main clause to complete it is an error known as a SENTENCE FRAGMENT.

descendant, ancestor

Do not confuse **descendant** and **ancestor**. Your **descendants** are your children, grandchildren, great-grandchildren, etc. Your **ancestors** are your parents, grandparents, great-grandparents, etc.

descent, decent, dissent

A downward movement or slope is a **descent**. Something acceptable or proper is **decent**. Difference of opinion or sentiment is **dissent**.

desert, dessert

The spelling is **desert** for "abandon", for "a dry region", and in *getting one's just **deserts***. Something sweet eaten at the end of a meal is **dessert**.

destruction, destroy

⚠ Warning: **destruction** and **destroy** begin with *de-*, not *di-*.

device, devise

A gadget or tool is a **device**. To plan carefully is to **devise**.

dice, die

Although historically **dice** is the plural of **die**, in modern standard English **dice** is both the singular and the plural, so that *Throw the **dice*** could refer to either one or more than one **die**.

die, dye

To perish is to **die** (**died**, **dying**); a device for stamping, cutting, or moulding is a **die**; a numbered cube is a **die**. The liquid used to colour hair or textiles is **dye**; to use such a liquid is to **dye** (**dyed**, **dyeing**).

die, dice

Although historically **die** is the singular of **dice**, in modern standard English **dice** is both the singular and the plural, so that *Throw the **dice*** could refer to either one or more than one **die**.

differ, defer
To disagree or to be different is to **differ**. To put something off is to **defer** it.

difference, deference
That which is not the same is **different**. Respect or consideration is **deference**: *In **deference** to one of the guests, who was a vegetarian, we did not serve meat.*

different, very different
Instead of saying that something is **different** or **very different**, try to use more precise and interesting adjectives to describe things:

> ***diverse**/**dissimilar**/**varying*** tastes
> ***contrasting**/**inconsistent**/**incompatible*** styles
> ***opposing**/**differing**/**disparate*** views
> *a **changed**/**altered**/**modified** form*
> *three **separate**/**distinct**/**discrete** categories*
> *a collection of **assorted**/**miscellaneous**/**various**/
>   **sundry** items*
> *her music is **unusual**/**distinctive**/
>   **unconventional***

different from/than
Although **different from** is often considered the most acceptable construction in sentences like *Cars are **different from** boats*, it is both common and acceptable to use **different than**, as in *Cars are **different than** boats*. **Different than** is even more widely accepted in comparisons where a clause rather than a noun follows **than**, as in *Donna is a **different** person **than** she was a year ago*, which is shorter than the alternative, *Donna is a **different** person **from** the one she was a year ago.*

diffuse, defuse

To spread or disperse is to **diffuse**: *The sunlight was diffused by the thin clouds*; something spread out is **diffuse**. You can **defuse** a bomb or a tense situation.

dingy, dinghy

Something dirty or gloomy is **dingy**. A small boat is a **dinghy**.

diphtheria, diphthong

⚠ Warning: do not forget the *h* after the *p* in the words **diphtheria** and **diphthong**.

direct object

G a noun, pronoun, or noun phrase that refers to a person or thing that is affected by the action of a verb, e.g. *him* in *She likes him*.

direct speech

G the reporting of speech by repeating the actual words of a speaker, for example: *"I'm going," she said*. In contrast, *She said that she was going* is REPORTED SPEECH.

disaster, disastrous

Note that the word **disastrous** does not contain the word **disaster**.

disc, disk

Disc is the usual Canadian spelling for a flat circular object (***disc**-shaped*, ***disc** brake*), the part of the spine (*slipped **disc***), and for audio and video recording terms (*compact **disc**, Mini **Disc**, laser **disc**, **disc** jockey*). However, **disk** is the usual Canadian spelling for computer storage devices other than *compact **disc***: *floppy **disk**; hard **disk**; optical **disk**; magnetic **disk**; **disk** drive*.

discover, discovery

The use of the words **discover** and **discovery** in

reference to European exploration of other continents is widely considered to be offensive to Aboriginal peoples. Rather than saying *The Vikings may have **discovered** Canada*, it would be better to say *The Vikings may have been the first Europeans to reach Canada*.

D

discreet, discrete
Someone who can keep a secret is **discreet**; **discreet** inquiries do not provoke curiosity. Separate or distinct things are **discrete**.

discus, discuss
The disc thrown as a sport is a **discus**. To talk over an issue is to **discuss** it.

dissect
⚠ Warning: **dissect** is spelled with two *s*'s.

dysfunction
⚠ Warning: **dysfunction** begins with *dys-*, not *dis-*.

disinterest
The use of **disinterest** to mean "lack of interest" is sometimes criticized, though it is more commonly used in this sense than in the sense "impartiality". The phrase *lack of interest* avoids both ambiguity and accusations of incorrect usage.

disinterested
In formal writing and speech, **disinterested** should not be used to mean "not interested, bored, uninterested". The most common sense of **disinterested** is "unbiased, impartial", as in *The case should be heard by a **disinterested** judge and jury*. Those who use **disinterested** to mean "uninterested" risk being misunderstood.

disk, disc
Disc is the usual Canadian spelling for a flat circular

object (***disc***-shaped, ***disc*** brake), the part of the spine (*slipped **disc***), and for audio and video recording terms (*compact **disc***, *Mini **Disc***, *laser **disc***, ***disc** jockey*). However, **disk** is the usual spelling in *floppy **disk***, *hard **disk***, *optical **disk***, *magnetic **disk***, and ***disk** drive*.

D

✗ dislexia, dislexic → **dyslexia, dyslexic** ✔
Warning: **dyslexia** and **dyslexic** begin with *dys-*, not *dis-*.

disperse, disburse
To scatter is to **disperse**. If you distribute money you **disburse** it.

dissent, descent
Difference of opinion or sentiment is **dissent**. A downward movement or slope is a **descent**.

distinct, distinctive
Do not confuse **distinct** and **distinctive**. **Distinct** refers to something that stands out as being different from its surroundings, while **distinctive** refers to a quality that distinguishes one thing from another. ***Distinct** red spots on the back of the beetle* tells you that the red spots stood out clearly or were easily distinguished, while ***distinctive** red spots on the back of the beetle* indicates that the red spots are what sets this beetle apart from other beetles.

✗ distruction, distroy → **destruction, destroy** ✔
Warning: **destruction** and **destroy** begin with *de-*, not *di-*.

don, dawn
The spelling is **don** for "a supervisor at a university residence" and for "to wear". The first light of morning is **dawn**.

double negatives

Sentences such as *I didn't do nothing* meaning "I didn't do anything" are ungrammatical. Sentences in which two negative elements are used to create a positive statement, as in *It was a slow but not unpleasant drive*, suggesting the drive was somewhat pleasant, are standard and acceptable.

douse, dowse

The usual Canadian spelling for "drench or soak" is **douse**. To search for water with a Y-shaped stick is to **dowse**.

drier, dryer

Something that is "more dry" is **drier**. **Dryer** is the usual Canadian spelling for something that dries.

dual, duel

Something with two parts or aspects is **dual**: *dual citizenship*. A conflict involving two parties is a **duel**.

due, duly

 Warning: **duly** is spelled without an *e*.

duel, dual

A conflict involving two parties is a **duel**. Something with two parts or aspects is **dual**: *dual citizenship*.

Dutchie, duchy

A square doughnut with raisins is a **Dutchie**. The territory of a duke or duchess is a **duchy**.

dying, dyeing

Perishing is **dying**. The process of colouring a fabric etc. is **dyeing**.

dysfunction

Warning: **dysfunction** begins with *dys-*, not *dis-*.

dyslexia
⚠ Warning: **dyslexia** begins with *dys-*, not *dis-*.

earn, urn
What you get paid is what you **earn**. A decorative container or vase is an **urn**.

East Indian
The term **South Asian** is now often preferred to **East Indian** as a general term designating the Indian subcontinent and its people.

easy, easily
The use of **easy** as an adverb is usually restricted to set phrases such as *Easy does it* and *Take it easy*. Outside of such expressions, the adverb **easily** is more standard: write *we beat them easily*, not *we beat them easy*.

ecstasy
⚠ Warning: **ecstasy** contains no *x* and ends in *-asy*, not *-acy*.

eek, eke
The shriek is spelled **eek**. The spelling is **eke** in *eke out*.

effect, affect
Sometimes people confuse the words **effect** and **affect**. **Effect**, especially in the phrase *have an effect on*, is a noun that means "a result or influence": *Alcohol has a very bad effect on drivers*. **Effect** is also a formal verb meaning "to achieve": *People lack confidence in their ability to effect change in society*. **Affect** is a verb that means "to have an influence on": *Alcohol affects drivers' concentration*.

elicit, illicit
To evoke a response or obtain an answer is to **elicit** them. Something secret or illegal is **illicit**.

ellipsis
For guidance on the use of the ellipsis see Appendix 1.

elude, allude
To evade something is to **elude** it. When you refer to
something you **allude** to it.

embarrass
⚠ Warning: in the word **embarrass** you double the *r* and
double the *s*.

eminently, imminently
Eminently means "notably" or "remarkably": *He came up
with an **eminently** melodic tune.* Something happening
imminently is about to happen.

ensure, insure
The usual Canadian spelling for "make certain" is **ensure**:
*Her job is to **ensure** that everyone is notified.* The usual
Canadian spelling for "secure payment in the event of a
loss" is **insure**: *I hope you **insured** your bike.*

entomology, etymology
The study of insects is **entomology**. The study of word
histories is **etymology**.

equally
The phrase **equally as** is redundant and should not be
used to make a comparison, as in *I enjoy books, but I find
movies **equally** as interesting.* It is correct to say either *I
enjoy books, but I find movies **equally** interesting* or *I find
movies as interesting as books.*

Eskimo
The word **Eskimo** is no longer used for the Aboriginal
people inhabiting northern Canada or their language. The
people are now referred to as **Inuit** (singular **Inuk**) and
their language is **Inuktitut**.

-ess

Gender-neutral words like *actor*, *heir*, *server*, and *flight attendant* are often preferred to "female" words ending in -**ess** (*actress*, *heiress*, *waitress*, *stewardess*), which, though still common, are often seen as old-fashioned and patronizing. Some nouns using -**ess** are still acceptable, however (*abbess*, *goddess*, and *princess*, for instance).

-ette

The use of the suffix -**ette** to form new feminine nouns is uncommon today and may be considered offensive, except in cases where it is used in a deliberately flippant manner, such as *bimbette* or *jockette*.

everyday, every day

Everyday is an adjective meaning "daily" or "commonplace": *Soon afterwards they resumed their everyday activities*, whereas **every day** means "each day" or "always": *It was something we had to do every day*.

everyone, every one

Everyone means "everybody", as in *Everyone has arrived*, whereas **every one** means "each person or thing in a given group", as in *Every one of them has arrived* or *Every one of these eggs is broken*.

exaggerate

⚠ Warning: in the word **exaggerate** you double the *g* but not the *r*.

exalt, exult

To praise people is to **exalt** them. To feel joy as a result of triumph or success is to **exult**.

exceed, accede

To be greater than or to surpass is to **exceed**. To agree to something or to take office is to **accede**.

✗ excelerate → accelerate ✔
Warning: **accelerate** starts with *accel-*, not *excel-*.

except, accept
A word that means "not including" is **except**. When you
receive something willingly you **accept** it.

exclamation mark
*For guidance on the use of the exclamation mark see Appendix
1.*

exercise
⚠ Warning: there is no *c* immediately following the *x* in
exercise.

exercise, exorcise
Physical activity is **exercise**; to use or apply something is
to **exercise** it: ***exercise*** *restraint*; ***exercise*** *a right*. To drive
out an evil spirit with prayers or magic is to **exorcise** it.

exhilarate
⚠ Warning: **exhilarate** is spelled with an *h*: ***exhil-***.

exorcise, exercise
To drive out an evil spirit with prayers or magic is to
exorcise it. Physical activity is **exercise**; to use or apply
something is to **exercise** it: ***exercise*** *restraint*; ***exercise*** *a
right*.

✗ exstasy → ecstasy ✔
Warning: **ecstasy** contains no *x* and ends in *-asy*, not *-acy*.

exulted, exalted
To have felt great joy is to have **exulted**. A position of
great importance is an ***exalted*** *position* or an ***exalted***
rank; **exalted** is also the spelling in *After the ballet she felt
alive and **exalted**.*

E

faint, feint

Something barely visible or audible is **faint**; if you lose consciousness, you **faint**. A move made to deceive an opponent is a **feint**.

fair, fare

Something done according to the rules is **fair**; **fair** is also used for blond hair or a clear sky; an exhibition is a **fair**. The money charged for a bus or cab ride is a **fare**; food or other things offered for consumption can also be called **fare**; something that does not succeed is said to *fare badly*.

fairy, ferry

A sprite is a **fairy**. A passenger boat is a **ferry**.

fare, fair

The money charged for a bus or cab ride is a **fare**; food or other things offered for consumption can also be called **fare**; something that does not succeed is said to *fare badly*. Something done according to the rules is **fair**; **fair** is also used for blond hair or a clear sky; an exhibition is a **fair**.

farther, further

Farther and **further** can both be used to describe physical distance: *We walked farther* (or *further*) *than I had expected*; *Lethbridge is farther* (or *further*) *than I thought*. Of the two, **further** is more likely to be used to mean "to a greater extent" (*Nothing could be further from the truth*). Only **further** is used to mean "in addition" (*We must decide when and, further, where to hold the meeting*), "additional" (*Please reply without further delay*), and "promote" (*He used them to further his own career*). Similarly, **farthest** and **furthest** are both used to describe physical distance (*She walked farthest* (or *furthest*); *She walked to the farthest* (or *furthest*) *point*), but **furthest** is more likely to be used to mean "to the greatest extent or degree" (*These are the people furthest removed from the political process*).

faun, fawn

A mythical creature that is half goat and half man is a **faun**. A young deer is a **fawn**; a light brown colour is **fawn**; if you behave obsequiously to someone, you **fawn** over them.

faze, phase

If something doesn't bother you, it doesn't **faze** you. Each stage of a process is a **phase**; to introduce something gradually is to *phase it in*.

February

 Warning: there is an *r* immediately after the *b* in **February**. **February** can be pronounced "FEB you ary" or "FEB roo ary".

feet, feat

The plural of *foot* is **feet**. An accomplishment is a **feat**.

feint, faint

A move made to deceive an opponent is a **feint**. Something barely visible or audible is **faint**. If you lose consciousness, you **faint**.

felony

The term **felony** is no longer used in Canadian law. Crimes in Canada are classified as **indictable offences** or **summary conviction offences**. **Felony** can still be used in a figurative sense, as in *Some reporters commit journalistic **felony** by unscrupulous or careless or lax reporting.*

ferry, fairy

A passenger boat is a **ferry**. A sprite is a **fairy**.

fewer, less

As a rule, do not use **less** with quantities that can be counted. Say *Simone has **fewer** dresses than I do* or *Doctors recommend we eat sweets **fewer** than five times a week.* You can use **less** with quantities of time, money, or distance that are regarded as wholes, as in *We have **less** than two weeks to finish our assignment* or *I have **less** than five dollars to spend on lunch*.

fiery
⚠ Warning: **fiery** is spelled with the *e* before the *r*.

filet, fillet
Filet is the spelling in *filet mignon*. The usual Canadian spelling for a fleshy boneless piece of meat is **fillet**; when you remove the bones from fish or meat and cut it into strips you **fillet** it.

Filipino, Pilipino, Philippine, Philippines
A person from the **Philippines** is a **Filipino**. Another word for the adjective *Filipino* is **Philippine**. The language of the *Filipinos* is **Pilipino**.

fillet, filet
The usual Canadian spelling for a fleshy boneless piece of meat is **fillet**; when you remove the bones from fish or meat and cut it into strips you **fillet** it. **Filet** is the spelling in *filet mignon*.

fin, Finn
An appendage on a fish is a **fin**. A person from Finland is a **Finn**.

finish, Finnish
To complete something is to **finish** it. Someone from Finland is **Finnish**.

fir, fur
The evergreen tree is a **fir**. An animal's coat of hair is its **fur**.

✗ firey → fiery ✔
Warning: **fiery** is spelled with the *e* before the *r*.

First Nations, First Peoples
The term **First Nations** refers only to Indian bands and does not include the Inuit or Metis. The term **First Peoples** includes Indians, Inuit, and Metis.

first person
G a set of pronouns and verb forms used by a speaker to refer to himself or herself, or to a group including himself or herself: *I am* is the first person singular of the present tense of the verb *to be*; *I, me, we* and *us* are first person pronouns.

F

✗ firy → fiery ✔
Warning: **fiery** is spelled with an *e* before the *r*.

flair, flare
Someone who is naturally talented at something has a **flair** for it; someone who is very stylish has **flair**. **Flare** is the spelling for a bright flame or the widening part of a skirt or pant leg; something that suddenly becomes active or intense is said to *flare up*.

flammable, inflammable
Both **flammable** and **inflammable** mean "easily set on fire". The opposite of **flammable** and **inflammable** is **non-flammable**.

flare, flair
Flare is the spelling for a bright flame or the widening part of a skirt or pant leg; something that suddenly becomes active or intense is said to *flare up*. Someone who is naturally talented at something has a **flair** for it; someone who is very stylish has **flair**.

flaunt, flout
Do not confuse **flaunt** with **flout**. To **flaunt** something means to "show off or display something arrogantly", as in *Angus is always flaunting his wealth*. To **flout** something

means to "disregard something openly", as in *Angus parks his car wherever he likes, **flouting** all parking regulations*.

flautist, flutist
Some people believe that **flautist** is the only correct word for a person who plays the flute. In fact, **flutist** is perfectly acceptable and more common than **flautist** in North American English.

flea, flee
The insect is a **flea**. To run away is to **flee**.

flew, flu, flue
The past tense of "fly" is **flew**. The illness is the **flu**. The part of a chimney is a **flue**.

floe, flow
A sheet of floating ice is a **floe**. To glide along like a river is to **flow**.

flour, flower
When you bake a cake or bread you use **flour**. The blossom of a plant is a **flower**.

**✗ flourescent, flouridate, flouride, flourine →
fluorescent, fluoridate, fluoride, fluorine ✔**
Warning: words like these are spelled with the *u* before the *o*.

flout, flaunt
Do not confuse **flout** with **flaunt**. To **flout** something means to "disregard something openly", as in *Angus parks his car wherever he likes, **flouting** all parking regulations*. To **flaunt** something means to "show off or display something arrogantly", as in *Angus is always **flaunting** his wealth*.

flow, floe
To glide along like a river is to **flow**. A sheet of floating ice is a **floe**.

flower, flour
The blossom of a plant is a **flower**. When you bake a cake or a loaf of bread you use **flour**.

flu, flue
The part of a chimney is a **flue**. The illness is the **flu**.

fluorescent, fluoridate, fluoride, fluorine
⚠ Warning: words like these are spelled with the *u* before the *o*.

F

flutist, flautist
Some people believe that **flautist** is the only correct word for "a flute player". In fact, **flutist** is perfectly acceptable and more common than **flautist** in North American English.

forbear, forebear
When you resist the urge to do something you **forbear** to do it. The usual Canadian spelling for an ancestor is **forebear**.

fore, four
The front part of something is the **fore**; something that gains a prominent position *comes to the **fore***. **Fore!** is what golfers shout to clear a fairway. The number is **four**.

foregoing, foregone, forgo
Do not confuse **forgo** with **foregoing** and **foregone**. To **forgo** something is to give it up or decide to do without it: *He's always **forgoing** dessert; the joys they had **forgone** when they decided to move away*. The words **foregoing** and **foregone** refer to something coming beforehand: *her **foregoing** remarks* (i.e. her previously mentioned remarks); *a **foregone** conclusion* (a conclusion which could have been predicted beforehand).

foresee
⚠ Warning: do not forget the *e* before the *s* in **foresee**.

foreword, forward
The introduction to a book is a **foreword**. The opposite of *backward* is **forward**.

forget, forgot, forgotten
Some people say *I haven't **forgot** about our meeting*, but it is better to say *I haven't **forgotten** about our meeting*.

F

forgo, foregoing, foregone
Do not confuse **forgo** with **foregoing** and **foregone**. To **forgo** something is to give it up or decide to do without it: *He's always **forgoing** dessert; the joys they had **forgone** when they decided to move away*. A predictable result is a ***foregone** conclusion*. In written passages, something just mentioned may be referred to as *the **foregoing***.

former
Former should only be used to refer to the first-mentioned of two things, as in *I like both lasagna and cannelloni, but I prefer the **former***. The use of **former** to refer to the first of three or more things, as in *I could take the train, plane, or bus—I'm leaning towards the **former** option* is considered incorrect by some people and is not recommended. It would be better to say either *—I'm favouring the train* or *—I'm leaning towards the first option*. See also LATTER.

✗ forsee → foresee ✔
Warning: do not forget the *e* before the *s* in **foresee**.

forth, fourth
A formal word for *forward* is **forth**. After *third* comes **fourth**.

forty
⚠ Warning: there is no *u* in **forty**.

forward, foreword
The opposite of *backward* is **forward**. The introduction to a book is a **foreword**.

foul, fowl
Something unpleasant or unfair is **foul**. A turkey is a type of **fowl**.

F

four, fore
The number is **four**. The front part of something is the **fore**; something that gains a prominent position *comes to the fore*. **Fore!** is what golfers shout to clear a fairway.

fourth, forth
After *third* comes **fourth**. A formal word for *forward* is **forth**.

✗ fourty → forty ✔
Warning: there is no *u* in **forty**.

fowl, foul
A turkey is a type of **fowl**. Something unpleasant or unfair is **foul**.

fragment
G a writing error where a dependent clause or a phrase is treated as if it were a complete sentence, separated from the independent clause to which it belongs by a period. Examples of fragments are the following:

> I didn't see the film. *Because I felt that it would be too violent for my taste.*
> It was a hilarious moment. *One that I shall never forget.*
> He gave me half his sandwich. *Being of a generous nature.*

frank, franc
To be candid or forthright is to be **frank**. The former French unit of money is the **franc**.

freeze, frieze

To become very cold is to **freeze**. A broad, sculpted or painted decoration on a wall is a **frieze**.

fryer, friar

A pot for frying is a **fryer**. A member of a religious order is a **friar**.

fulsome

Because **fulsome** can mean either "excessively flattering" or "abundant", a sentence like *Desmond showered the president with **fulsome** praise* can be ambiguous: is Desmond's praise abundant but genuine or insincere? Avoid using **fulsome** unless it is obvious from the context which sense is intended, as in *Desmond, sincerely moved by the president's presentation, showered her with **fulsome** praise* or *Desmond, who had a reputation for obsequiousness, showered the president with **fulsome** praise*.

fur, fir

An animal's coat of hair is its **fur**. The evergreen tree is a **fir**.

further, farther

Further and **farther** can both be used to describe physical distance: *We walked **further** (or **farther**) than I had expected; Lethbridge is **further** (or **farther**) than I thought*. Of the two, **further** is more likely to be used to mean "to a greater extent" (*Nothing could be **further** from the truth*). Only **further** is used to mean "in addition" (*We must decide when and, **further**, where to hold the meeting*), "additional" (*Please reply without **further** delay*), and "promote" (*He used them to **further** his own career*). Similarly, **furthest** and **farthest** are both used to describe physical distance (*She walked **furthest** (or **farthest**); She walked to the **furthest** (or **farthest**) point*), but **furthest** is more likely to be used to mean "to the greatest extent or degree" (*These are the people **furthest** removed from the political process*).

furthest, farthest
The form **farthest** is used especially with reference to physical distance, although **furthest** is preferred by many even in this sense.

fury, furry
Rage is **fury**. Something with fur is **furry**.

gage, gauge
Gauge is the usual Canadian spelling for *gauge a reaction, temperature **gauge***, and *12-**gauge** shotgun*. (**Gage** is the US spelling in these senses.)

gait, gate
A **gait** is a manner of walking. A barrier that can be opened is a **gate**; an obstacle on a slalom course is a **gate**.

gallop, Gallup poll
A horse's pace is a **gallop**. The poll is a **Gallup** poll.

✗ garantee **→** guarantee **✔**
Warning: There is a *u* before the *a* in **guarantee**.

gate, gait
A barrier that can be opened is a **gate**; an obstacle on a slalom course is a **gate**. The way a person walks is their **gait**.

gel, jell
A semi-solid substance is a **gel**; some people **gel** their hair. The usual Canadian spelling is **jell** in *Our ideas are beginning to **jell***, *This team is really starting to **jell***, and *The liquid will **jell** overnight in the fridge*.

Gentile, genteel

A non-Jewish person is a **Gentile**. Someone who is polite or refined is **genteel**.

gerund

G a noun formed from a verb, ending in -*ing*, and designating an action or state, e.g. *smoking is bad for you.*

gild, guild

To cover something with gold is to **gild** it. The usual Canadian spelling for an association of people with related jobs or interests is **guild**.

gilt, guilt

Something covered with gold is **gilt**. The opposite of innocence is **guilt**.

gladiolus

Note that **gladiolus** is a singular noun (the plural being either **gladioli** or **gladioluses**): there is no word "gladiola".

glamour, glamorous

Note that in Canada **glamour** usually has a *u* immediately following the *o*, but **glamorous** never does.

gofer, gopher

A person who runs errands is a **gofer**. The small animal is a **gopher**.

gone, went

Never say *I should have went.* The correct form is *I should have **gone**.*

gonna

Gonna is not considered standard English and should not be used in careful writing and speech.

good, very good

Instead of saying that something is **good** or **very good**, try to use more precise and interesting adjectives to describe things:

> a **talented/skilful/superb** athlete
> a **masterful/proficient/distinguished/brilliant** musician
> an **enjoyable/entertaining/exciting/engrossing** movie
> the food here is **delicious/appetizing/tasty**
> a **suitable/fitting/appropriate** response
> his excuse was **valid/legitimate/acceptable**
> an **honest/honourable/admirable** woman
> a **generous/benevolent/gracious/obliging** host
> a **well-behaved/polite/well-mannered** child
> a **reliable/dependable/trustworthy** employee
> a **hard-working/keen/conscientious/diligent** student
> our **close/intimate/dear/valued** friends

When referring to pleasant weather, you can use words like: **fair, mild, clear, calm,** or **tranquil.**

gopher, gofer

The small animal is a **gopher**. A person who runs errands is a **gofer**.

gorilla, guerrilla

The large ape is the **gorilla**. A member of a small, independent army is a **guerrilla**.

government

⚠ Warning: do not forget the *n* immediately after the *r* in **government**: the first part of the word is *govern*.

Governor General

Note that the plural of **Governor General** is **Governors General**.

great, grate

Something very good is **great**. To shred, rub, or scrape something is to **grate** it; something annoying **grates** on you; the metal rack for holding logs in a fireplace is a **grate**.

grisly, gristly, grizzly

Something horrible or gruesome is **grisly**. Meat containing tough, inedible bits is **gristly**. The large brown bear is a **grizzly**.

G

✘ guage → gauge ✔

Warning: *u* follows *a* in **gauge**.

guarantee

⚠ Warning: There is a *u* before the *a* in **guarantee**.

guild, gild

The usual Canadian spelling for an association of people with related jobs or interests is **guild**. To cover something with gold is to **gild** it.

guilt, gilt

The opposite of innocence is **guilt**. Something covered with gold is **gilt**.

gyp

Some people object to **gyp** because they feel it is related to the word *gypsy*, although this has not been proven. For this reason and because it is considered slang, it should be avoided in writing and speech. You can use words like **cheat**, **swindle**, **shortchange**, or **fleece** instead.

hail, hale

Frozen rain falling in pellets is **hail**; when you wave to a cab driver or a friend, or when you commend someone, you **hail** them. To be strong and healthy is to be **hale**.

hair, hare

What grows on the head is **hair**. The animal resembling a large rabbit is a **hare**; a rash or foolish idea is **hare-brained**.

hairy, harry

To have much hair is to be **hairy**. To harass or annoy people is to **harry** them.

hale, hail

To be strong and healthy is to be **hale**. Frozen rain falling in pellets is **hail**; when you wave to a cab driver or a friend, or when you commend someone, you **hail** them.

hall, haul

A corridor or large room is a **hall**. To drag something is to **haul** it; a long distance is a *long haul*.

handicraft, handiwork

⚠ Warning: the words **handicraft** and **handiwork** are spelled with an *i*, not with a *y*.

hang, hung, hanged

Note that while the past of most senses of **hang** is **hung**, the past for the sense "suspend from a rope by the neck until dead" is **hanged**: *The leader of the rebellion was hanged in a public execution; When they hanged the notorious Captain Kidd, the rope broke.*

hanger, hangar

A building that houses airplanes is a **hangar**. A coat is hung on a **hanger**.

harass

Harass can be pronounced with the stress on the first or second syllable. The pronunciation with the stress on the second syllable, "huh RASS", is the more common one and is perfectly acceptable, despite being considered incorrect by some people. Harass is spelled with only one *r*.

hardly

Words like **hardly**, **scarcely**, and **barely** should not be used with negative constructions, as in *I can't hardly wait for the weekend*. It is correct to say *I can **hardly** wait for the weekend*, *I can **scarcely** believe my eyes*, or *I can **barely** see with these new glasses*.

hare, hair

The animal is a **hare**. What grows on the head is **hair**.

✗ harrass → harass ✔

Warning: **harass** is spelled with only one *r*.

hart, heart

A male deer is a **hart**. The organ that pumps blood through the body is the **heart**.

have: could/should/would have

Use **have**, not **of**, in expressions like **might have**, **could have**, **would have**, and **should have**: *I should **have** been more careful* (not *I should of been more careful*).

hawk, hock

The bird of prey is the **hawk**; **hawk** also means "clear the throat" or "go around offering goods for sale". To deposit an item with a pawnbroker is to **hock** it; the joint of an animal's hind leg is the **hock**.

✗ hayday → heyday ✔

Warning: the first part of **heyday** is spelled with an *e*.

he

The use of **he** to refer to a person of unspecified sex, as in *Every child needs to know that **he** is loved*, is often criticized as sexist. Suitable alternatives include *Every child needs to* *know that **he** or **she** is loved* and *All children need to know that **they** are loved*. In sentences in which **he** appears after *everyone, anyone,* or *someone,* as in *Everyone can do whatever **he** likes,* **he** can again be replaced by **he** or **she**: *Everyone can do whatever **he** or **she** likes*. This option sometimes results in sentences that are long or awkward. Another possibility is to use **they**: *Everyone can do whatever **they** like*. This use of **they** may be considered incorrect by some, however; see THEY.

heal, heel

To recover is to **heal**. Part of the foot is the **heel**; dogs are taught to **heel** when walking; a leaning boat is said to **heel**; someone who behaves inconsiderately is a **heel**.

hear, here

To detect sound is to **hear**. The opposite of *there* is **here**.

heart, hart

The organ that pumps blood through the body is the **heart**. A male deer is a **hart**.

heel, heal

Part of the foot is the **heel**; dogs are taught to **heel** when walking; a leaning boat is said to **heel**; someone who behaves inconsiderately is a **heel**. To recover is to **heal**.

✗ heirarchy, heiroglyph → hierarchy, hieroglyph ✔

Warning: the *e* follows the *i* in **hierarchy** and **hieroglyph**.

henceforth

Note that **henceforth** means "from this time onward": ***Henceforth** all job openings will be posted internally first;* it does not mean "up to now".

her, she

The use of **her** instead of **she** after the verb *to be,* as in *It's* *her on the phone*, is now considered acceptable in writing as well as speech. In sentences like *It is **she** who keeps calling*, however, **she** must be used instead of **her**. To avoid sounding excessively formal, such a sentence could be reworded ***She's** the one who keeps calling*, which is much more natural. See also THAN.

herb
Herb can be pronounced either with the *h*-sound (*a **herb***) or without (*an **herb***).

herd, heard
A group of cattle is a **herd**. The past tense of *hear* is **heard**.

here, hear
The opposite of *there* is **here**. To detect sound is to **hear**.

hers
⚠ Warning: **hers** is not spelled with an apostrophe.

herself
Do not misuse **herself**. Sentences like *Her mother, her father, and **herself** are home for the holidays* and *They were very kind to her husband and **herself*** are not recommended. It is better to say *Her mother, her father, and she are home for the holidays* and *They were very kind to her and her husband*. Reserve **herself** for reflexive uses like *She helped **herself** to a drink* or emphatic ones like *She **herself** was once an artist like you*.

hew, hue
To cut or chop something is to **hew** it. A colour or shade is a **hue**; **hue** is also the spelling in ***hue** and cry*.

heyday

⚠ Warning: the first part of **heyday** is spelled with an *e*.

hierarchy, hieroglyph

⚠ Warning: don't forget the *e* immediately following the *i* in **hierarchy** and **hieroglyph**.

him, he

The use of **him** instead of **he** after the verb "to be", as in *It's **him** on the phone*, is now considered acceptable in writing as well as speech. In sentences like *It is **he** who keeps calling*, however, **he** must be used instead of **him**. To avoid sounding excessively formal, such a sentence could be reworded ***He's** the one who keeps calling*, which is much more natural. See also THAN.

himself

Do not misuse **himself**. Sentences like *Both Gigi and himself have come* and *They brought water for his horse and himself* are not recommended. It is better to say *He and Gigi have come* and *They brought water for him and his horse*. Reserve **himself** for reflexive uses like *He helped **himself** to a drink* or emphatic ones like *He **himself** was once an artist like you*.

Hindi, Hindu

Hindi refers to a language of India, while **Hindu** refers to Hinduism: *a **Hindi** text* is a text in the Hindi language, while *a **Hindu** text* is a religious text on Hinduism.

hippy, hippie

Hippie is the usual Canadian spelling for a youth who rejected traditional social values in the 1960s and 1970s. **Hippy** describes someone with large hips.

hirarchy, hiroglyph → **hierarchy, hieroglyph** ✔

✗ Warning: **hierarchy** and **hieroglyph** are spelled *hier-*.

his

The use of **his** to refer to a person of unspecified sex, as in *Every student must do **his** homework*, is often criticized as sexist. Suitable alternatives include *Every student must do*

his or *her* homework and *All students must do **their**
homework*, or simply *All students must do homework*. The
use of the plural pronoun **their** following a singular
noun, as in *Every student must do **their** homework*, is
considered incorrect by some, but is becoming more and
more accepted in writing and speech. See THEIR.

hoard, horde
A large supply of money, food, or other valuable objects is
a **hoard**. A crowd of people is a **horde**.

H

hoarse, horse
Someone with a sore throat and a raspy voice is **hoarse**.
The animal is a **horse**.

hock, hawk
To deposit an item with a pawnbroker is to **hock** it; the
joint of an animal's hind leg is the **hock**. The bird of prey
is a **hawk**; **hawk** also means "clear the throat" or "go
around offering goods for sale".

hole, whole
An opening is a **hole**. Something complete is **whole**.

holey, holy
Something with holes is **holey**. Something associated
with God or religion is **holy**.

homogenous, homogeneous
The use of **homogenous** to mean "all of the same kind"
or "uniform" is considered incorrect by many people and
is best avoided; the correct word is **homogeneous**.

honorary, honourary
Unlike the word **honour**, the word **honorary** is rarely
spelled with a *u*. In fact, only in Canada is it ever spelled
with a *u*: everyone in the rest of the world (including
Britain) always spells it as **honorary**.

hopefully

Hopefully is used much more commonly in written and spoken English to mean "it is to be hoped that", as in **Hopefully** *Sujit will invite us*, than to mean "in a hopeful manner", as in *We waited* **hopefully** *for Sujit to invite us*. Nevertheless, some people object very strongly to the first use. The case against it is weak, but it may be safer not to use a sentence like **Hopefully** *Sujit will invite us* in formal writing to avoid fierce criticism. An acceptable alternative is *I* (or *we*) **hope that** *Sujit will invite us*.

horde, hoard

A crowd of people is a **horde**. A large supply of money, food, or other valuable objects is a **hoard**.

horse, hoarse

The animal is a **horse**. Someone with a sore throat and a raspy voice is **hoarse**.

hostel, hostile

A place providing temporary accommodation is a **hostel**. Someone who is unfriendly is **hostile**.

hottie, haughty

A **hottie** is someone who is sexually attractive. **Haughty** is used to describe someone proud and arrogant.

however

Be careful to use correct punctuation when you use **however**. The following five examples are all correct:

> *I wanted to go;* **however**, *he didn't.*
> (make sure you use a semicolon, not a comma, before **however** and a comma after it)
> *The deficit has been a concern for Canadians for years.*
> **However,** *the government has decided to spend its budget surplus on tax reduction.*
> (don't forget the comma after **however**)

*Problems in such areas, **however**, may be alleviated by increased ventilation.*

*He wasn't expecting to see a bear, **however**.*

(since in both these examples **however** is not introducing a new clause containing a subject and verb, it is just set off from the rest of the sentence by commas)

***However** inconvenient it is for you to visit her every day, you still must do it.*

(here, **however** comes before an adjective and is therefore not followed by a comma)

H

Hudson Bay, Hudson's Bay
Note that the body of water is **Hudson Bay**, but the spelling is **Hudson's Bay** in **Hudson's Bay** Company and **Hudson's Bay** blanket.

hue, hew
A colour or shade is a **hue**; **hue** is also the spelling in **hue** and cry. To cut or chop something is to **hew** it.

huge
A minority of Canadian speakers do not pronounce the *h* in words like **huge**, **human**, **humane**, **humanitarian**, and **humour**. Although this is uncommon, it is acceptable.

humerus, humorous
The bone in the arm is the **humerus**. Something funny is **humorous**.

humorous, humourous
Unlike the word **humour**, the word **humorous** is rarely spelled with a *u* before the *r*. In fact, only in Canada is it ever spelled with a *u*: everyone in the rest of the world (including Britain) always spells it as **humorous**.

humus, hummus
Decomposed plant matter in soil is **humus**. The spicy chickpea paste eaten as a dip is **hummus**.

hung, hanged
Note that while **hung** is the past tense and past participle of most senses of **hang**, the past for the sense "suspend from a rope by the neck until dead" is **hanged**: *The leader of the rebellion was **hanged** in a public execution; When they **hanged** the notorious Captain Kidd, the rope broke.*

hurdle, hurtle
An obstacle is a **hurdle**. To move wildly at a dangerous speed is to **hurtle**.

hyperthermia, hypothermia
Do not confuse **hyperthermia** with **hypothermia**. **Hyperthermia** is a condition in which a person's body temperature is above normal. **Hypothermia** is a condition in which a person's body temperature is below normal.

hyphen
For guidance on the use of the hyphen see Appendix 1.

hypocrisy
Note that **hypocrisy** ends in -*isy*, not -*acy*.

I, me
Never use **I** in sentences like *The teacher spoke to my father and I, The bus picked up my sister and I,* or *just between you and I.* In all these cases **I** should be replaced by **me**: *The teacher spoke to my father and **me**; The bus picked up my sister and **me**; just between you and **me**.* To know whether to use **I** or **me**, determine which form would be appropriate if you were the only one mentioned: Just as you would say *The teacher spoke to **me*** (and not *The teacher*

spoke to I), the correct form with *my father* is *The teacher spoke to **my father and me***. Similarly, because you would say ***I** went to see the teacher* (and not *Me went to see the teacher*), the correct form with *my father* is ***My father and I** went to see the teacher*.

idiosyncrasy
Note that **idiosyncrasy** ends in *-asy*, not *-acy*.

idle, idol
Someone who is lazy or inactive is **idle**; something pointless or worthless is also **idle**: ***idle** speculation*; ***idle** gossip*. An object of worship is an **idol**.

illicit, elicit
Something secret or illegal is **illicit**. To evoke a response or obtain an answer is to **elicit** them.

illusion, allusion
A false impression or a picture that deceives one's eyes is an **illusion**. When you make an indirect or passing reference to something you are making an **allusion**.

illusive, elusive
Don't confuse **illusive** with **elusive**. Something unreal like an illusion is **illusive**: *the tragedy behind our neighbours' **illusive** happiness*. Something hard to catch, obtain, or achieve is **elusive**: *We hoped to catch the **elusive** brook trout*.

immanent, imminent
Something present everywhere or inherent is **immanent**. Something about to happen is **imminent**.

imminently, eminently
Something happening **imminently** is about to happen. **Eminently** means "notably" or "remarkably": *He came up with an **eminently** melodic tune*.

impact

Impact is often used to mean "affect or influence", as in *The weather will **impact** on how long it takes to drive to the cottage* and *How are the cuts to welfare **impacting** low-income families?* Such uses sound jargony and can often be replaced to advantage with **affect**, as in *How are the cuts to welfare **affecting** low-income families?*

imperative

G the mood of a verb expressing a command, e.g. *wait!*

imply, infer

Imply should not be confused with **infer**. **Imply** means "to suggest indirectly", as in *I didn't tell Sonja I was angry but I **implied** it and I think she understood.* **Infer** means "to reach an opinion based on available information or evidence", as in *From these statistics our researchers **inferred** a connection between smoking and heart disease* or *From your enthusiastic response, I **infer** that you did indeed enjoy the movie.* The use of **infer** to mean **imply**, as in *I didn't tell Sonja I was angry, but I **inferred** it*, is generally considered wrong.

more importantly

Some people consider it incorrect to use **more importantly** instead of **more important** in sentences like *Paolo brought the party hats and the balloons and, **more importantly**, the cake.* However, **more importantly** is overwhelmingly more common than **more important** in this kind of construction and is perfectly acceptable.

indefinite article

G a word (*a* or *an* in English) preceding a noun and implying lack of specificity, as in *bought me a book*; *government is an art.*

indefinite pronoun

G a pronoun indicating a person, amount, etc., without being definite or particular, e.g. *any, some, anyone.*

independent clause

G a clause that is able to stand alone as a complete sentence.

Indian

The use of **Indian** to refer to the indigenous people of North and South America has declined recently because it is thought to reflect Columbus's mistaken idea that he had landed in India in 1492. However, in Canada it is still common in the usage of many Aboriginal people and embedded in legislation that is still in effect. It is also the only clear way to distinguish among the three general categories of Canadian Aboriginal people (**Indians**, Inuit, and Metis), and is therefore acceptable.

indirect object

G a person or thing affected by a verbal action but not primarily acted on, e.g. *him* in *give him the book*.

indirect question

G a question in reported speech, e.g. *they asked who I was*.

indirect speech

G (also **indirect discourse**, **reported speech**) a description of a speaker's words as opposed to a direct quotation, with the necessary changes of person, tense, etc., e.g. *she said that she would go* instead of *she said, "I will go"* (opposite DIRECT SPEECH).

inequity, iniquity

Unfairness or inequality is **inequity**. Wickedness or immorality is **iniquity**.

infer, imply

Infer should not be used to mean **imply**. **Infer** means "to reach an opinion based on available information or evidence", as in *From these statistics our researchers* ***inferred*** *a connection between smoking and heart disease* or *From your enthusiastic response, I* ***infer*** *that you did indeed* *enjoy the movie*. **Imply** means "to suggest indirectly", as in *I didn't tell Sonja I was angry but I implied it and I think she understood*. The use of **infer** to mean **imply**, as in *I didn't tell Sonja I was angry, but I **inferred** it*, is generally considered wrong.

infinitive
G the basic form of a verb, such as *be* or *run*, used either by itself, as *swim* in *She can swim,* or with *to* as in *She likes to swim*. See also SPLIT INFINITIVE.

inflammable, flammable
Both **inflammable** and **flammable** mean "easily set on fire". The opposite of **inflammable** and **flammable** is *non-flammable*.

ingenious, ingenuous, ingenuity
Ingenious should not be confused with **ingenuous**. **Ingenious** means "clever at inventing, resourceful", as in *Willy devised an **ingenious** science experiment*. **Ingenuous** means "open, frank, innocent", as in *How was Lisa to know that her **ingenuous** admission to liking Edgar would result in months of teasing from her friends?* **Ingenuity** is related to **ingenious**, not to **ingenuous**, and thus means "cleverness".

iniquity, inequity
Wickedness or immorality is **iniquity**. Unfairness or inequality is **inequity**.

in memoriam
⚠ Warning: **in memoriam** ends in *-am*, not *-um*.

innocuous
⚠ Warning: **innocuous** is spelled with two *n*'s.

inoculate
⚠ Warning: **inoculate** is spelled with one *n*.

in spite

⚠ Warning: the phrase **in spite** is always spelled as two words.

insure, ensure

The usual Canadian spelling for "secure payment in the event of a loss" is **insure**: *I hope you **insured** your bike.* The usual Canadian spelling for "make certain" is **ensure**: *Her job is to **ensure** that everyone is notified.*

interjection

G an exclamation, especially as a part of speech, e.g. *hey!, dear me!*

interrogative adjective

G an adjective (*which, whose*) that asks a question.

interrogative adverb

G an adverb (*where, when, why,* or *how*) that asks a question.

interrogative pronoun

G a pronoun (*who, whom, whose, which,* or *what*) that asks a question.

intransitive

G (of a verb or sense of a verb) that does not take or require a direct object (whether expressed or implied), e.g. *look* in *Look at the sky* (opposite TRANSITIVE).

invigorate

⚠ Warning: **invigorate** is never spelled with a *u* after the *o* the way **vigour** is.

ironic

Ironic is used to describe a comment, facial expression, or gesture that is used to express the opposite of what it usually means, as in *"Ha ha, very funny,"* was Roger's ***ironic*** *reply to Angie's joke about his new boots* or *Alicia looked at the D- on her essay and gave an **ironic** smile.* It is also used to describe a situation or event that happens in a completely opposite way to what one would have expected, as in *It is **ironic** that Maeve became a teacher, since she always hated school when she was a girl*. **Ironic** should not be used to describe a state of affairs that is mildly coincidental or paradoxical. Uses such as *It's ironic that it's sunny since they said it was going to rain on the news* or *It's ironic that you should mention Carl: I was just thinking about him* are not recommended.

irony
Irony is the expression of meaning with words or gestures that usually mean the opposite, as in *"That was smart," said Lydia, with **irony**, to James, who had just locked his keys in the car*. It is also a situation or event that seems deliberately contrary to what one expects, as in *The **irony** is that although Simone has worked all her life for the Humane Society, she has never liked animals*. **Irony** should not be used for any state of affairs that is mildly odd, coincidental, or paradoxical, as in *The irony is that we've been co-workers for five years and only just realized that we live on the same street*.

irrespective, regardless
Note that there is no such word as *irregardless*; appropriate alternatives include **regardless** and **irrespective**: *We'll go **regardless** of the weather; My constituents expect all their politicians, **irrespective** of political stripe or political agenda, to work together to improve their lives*.

isle, aisle
An island is an **isle**. A passageway is an **aisle**.

its, it's
Its should not be confused with **it's**. **Its**, meaning "belonging to it", does not have an apostrophe: *The dog wagged **its** tail*. The apostrophe is used only in the short form of **it is** or **it has**: ***It's** raining; **It's** been nice knowing you*.

-ize, -ise

The long-standing Canadian practice is to use **-ize** to form verbs: *Canadianize, economize*. This form is etymologically closer than **-ise** to the suffix's Greek and Latin roots, and has long been used throughout the English-speaking world, including Great Britain. The recent preference for **-ise** among the British is no reason for Canadians to abandon their well-established practice of using **-ize**. (Note that some verbs are always written with **-ise**, e.g. *advertise, advise, surprise*.)

jam, jamb

The spelling is **jam** for a fruit preserve and to squeeze or wedge. Part of a door frame is a **jamb**.

jean, gene

Denim pants are **jeans**. Part of a chromosome is a **gene**.

jell, gel

The usual Canadian spelling is **jell** in *Our ideas are beginning to **jell**, This team is really starting to **jell**,* and *The liquid will **jell** overnight in the fridge*. A semi-solid substance is a **gel**; *Some people **gel** their hair*.

junkie, junky

The usual Canadian spelling for an addict is **junkie**. Something like junk is **junky**.

karat, carat

The purity of gold is measured in **karats**. Diamonds are measured in **carats**.

Kashmir, cashmere

A region of South Asia is **Kashmir**. The spelling is **cashmere** for the soft wool.

kernel, colonel

The central part of something is a **kernel**. A military officer is a **colonel**.

key, quay

What opens a lock is a **key**. A place in a harbour where boats are loaded and unloaded is a **quay**.

kind

Expressions like *these kind* and *those sort* are ungrammatical. The recommended forms are **this** (or **that**) **kind**, **these** (or **those**) **kinds**. In Canadian English, when **kind** is singular, the noun following tends to be singular: *this **kind** of car; that **kind** of person*. When **kind** is made plural, the noun following it tends to be plural also: *these **kinds** of cars; those **kinds** of people*.

knit, nit

To work with wool is to **knit**; the spelling is **knit** in *to **knit** one's brow*. The eggs of lice are **nits**. Someone overly fussy is a **nitpicker**.

lama, llama

A Tibetan Buddhist monk is a **lama**. The camel-like animal is a **llama**.

latter

Latter should only be used to refer to the last-mentioned of two things, as in *I like both vanilla and chocolate, but I prefer the **latter***. The use of **latter** to refer to the last of three or more things, as in *We could see a movie, go out for dinner, or catch a hockey game—I'd most enjoy the latter* is considered incorrect by some people and is not recommended. It would be better to say either —*I'm leaning towards catching a hockey game* or —*I'm leaning towards the last option*. See also FORMER.

lay, lie

The following examples are considered incorrect: *Perhaps you should lay down for a while* (correct form is **lie**); *The dog was laying on the floor* (correct form is **lying**); *She lay the blanket over the sleeping baby* (correct form is **laid**); *She* *had laid on the couch for hours* (correct form is **lain**); *We have lain a clever plan* (correct form is **laid**).

leach, leech
Soil that has lost its nutrients has been **leached**. A bloodsucker or someone who lives off others is a **leech**.

lead, led
Lead is not the past tense of *to lead*—the past tense is **led**: *They **led** the league for half the season before slumping.* The metal is **lead**.

leak, leek
A hole through which something escapes is a **leak**. The vegetable is a **leek**.

learn
The use of **learn** to mean "teach" is unacceptable in spoken and written English except in humorous and very informal contexts and phrases, such as *That'll **learn** you!*

led, lead
The past tense of *to lead* is **led**. The metal is **lead**.

leech, leach
A bloodsucker or someone who lives off others is a **leech**. Soil that has lost its nutrients has been **leached**.

leek, leak
The vegetable is a **leek**. A hole through which something escapes is a **leak**.

less, fewer
As a rule, do not use **less** with quantities that can be counted. Say *Simone has **fewer** dresses than I do* or *Doctors recommend we eat sweets **fewer** than five times a week.* You can use **less** with quantities of time, money, or distance that are regarded as wholes, as in *We have **less** than two*

weeks to finish our assignment or *I have **less** than five dollars to spend on lunch.*

lest
Lest is a formal word meaning "so that (something) does not happen". The verb following **lest** is usually in the subjunctive mood, which means that it is identical to the infinitive: *The prisoner is being kept under surveillance **lest** he try to escape* or *I must speak slowly **lest** I be misunderstood.*

levee, levy
A reception or embankment is a **levee**. A collection is a **levy**.

liar, lyre
Someone who tells a lie is a **liar**. The musical instrument is a **lyre**.

licence, license
The usual Canadian spelling for the noun is **licence**, as in **licence** *plate* and *driver's* **licence**. The usual Canadian spelling for the verb is **license**: *an agreement to **license** the merchandise.*

lie, lay
The following examples are considered incorrect: *Perhaps you should lay down for a while* (correct form is **lie**); *The dog was laying on the floor* (correct form is **lying**); *She lay the blanket over the baby* (correct form is **laid**); *She had laid on the couch for hours* (correct form is **lain**); *We have lain a clever plan* (correct form is **laid**).

lieutenant
Many Canadians object to pronouncing **lieutenant** "loo TENNANT", regarding this pronunciation as American. However, outside of the Armed Forces, it is probably somewhat more common among Canadians

than "lef TENNANT", except in the word **Lieutenant-Governor**, where usage is more equally divided.

lightening, lightning
The act of making something lighter or brighter is **lightening**. A bright flash during a thunderstorm is **lightning**.

like, as
Although it is quite common in casual speech to use comparisons such as *He holds his guitar **like** Rosa does*, and *They were playing **like** they were professionals*, in formal contexts **like** should not be used when the comparison is being made to a statement with a verb in it (statements such as "Rosa *does*" and "they *were* professionals" in the examples above). **Like** would only be appropriate if the sentences were *He holds his guitar **like** Rosa*, and *They were playing like professionals*. The sentences could also be rewritten using **as** or **as if** instead of **like**: *He holds his guitar **as** Rosa does*; *They were playing **as if** they were professionals*.

liniment
⚠ Warning: the vowel in the second syllable of **liniment** is an *i*, not an *a*.

links, lynx
A chain is composed of **links**; golf is played on the **links**. The cat is a **lynx**.

liqueur, liquor
Liqueur, pronounced "li CURE", refers only to sweet flavoured alcohol such as Irish cream, amaretto, etc.; the general word for distilled alcohol, such as brandy, gin, whisky, vodka, etc., is **liquor**, pronounced "LICKER".

lite, light
The adjective **lite** is used only to describe low-fat or low-

sugar versions of food (and, by analogy, anything lacking substance); the standard spelling of the word meaning "not heavy" or "not dark" is **light**.

literal, literally

In writing and formal speech, do not use **literal** and **literally** simply to add emphasis, as in *It was a **literal** flood of tears* and *Mamud ran like a jet, **literally***—in these sentences the expressions *flood* and *like a jet* are not being used **literally** (i.e. they are not being used with their primary meanings), but *figuratively*.

llama, lama

The camel-like animal is a **llama**. A Buddhist monk is a **lama**.

load, lode

Something carried is a **load**. A vein of ore or a rich supply source is a **lode** or **motherlode**.

lock, loch

A secure fastener is a **lock**. A Scottish lake is a **loch**: *Loch Ness*.

long-ago, long ago

Note the difference in spelling between ***long-ago** events* and *events that happened **long ago***. There is no hyphen when the latter kind of structure is used.

long-dead, long dead

Note the difference in spelling between *a **long-dead** soldier* and *a soldier who is **long dead***. There is no hyphen when the latter kind of structure is used.

long-term, long term

Note the difference in spelling between ***long-term** plans* and *plans for the **long term***. There is no hyphen when the latter kind of structure is used.

loonie, loony

The coin is a **loonie**. A silly or mad person is a **loony**.

loose, lose

The opposite of *tight* is **loose**; if you release something you **loose** it: *loosed the dogs on them*. You can **lose** money, weight, a game, a glove, your job, your temper, or your balance.

loot, lute

Stolen objects or recently-obtained goodies are **loot**. The musical instrument is a **lute**.

lose, loose

You can **lose** money, weight, a game, a glove, your job, your temper, or your balance. The opposite of *tight* is **loose**; if you release something you **loose** it: *loosed the dogs on them*.

lots, a lot

Instead of saying that there is **lots** or **a lot** of something, try to use more precise and interesting terms:

> her health is **a great deal**/**much** better
> **many**/**a great many**/**a large number of** people came
>   to the party
> I go to Stuttgart **frequently**/**often**

A lot is always spelled as two words, not one.

loud, loudly

Loud and **loudly** can both be used as adverbs to describe an action. **Loudly** is the usual form, but **loud** is also correct, especially in informal language: *The audience laughed **loudly** at the joke; Do you have to play that music so **loud**?; You'll have to speak **louder**—I can't hear you.*

luxuriant, luxurious

Do not confuse **luxuriant** and **luxurious**. The word **luxuriant** refers to lush growth of plants or hair. **Luxurious** refers to luxury.

mackintosh, McIntosh

A British term for a raincoat is **mackintosh**. The apple is a **McIntosh**.

mad, very mad

Instead of saying that someone is **mad** or **very mad**, try to use more precise and interesting adjectives to describe people:

> *Angry demonstrators protested outside the building.*
> *I was **annoyed** at her for hanging up on me.*
> *I was **cross** with him for being late.*
> *He became **enraged** when the other children teased him.*
> *After an hour of trying to assemble the barbecue, I became **exasperated** and gave up.*
> *Passengers grew **frustrated** as the delay continued.*
> *The more they argued, the more **furious** they became.*
> *Workers were **incensed** by the arbitrator's decision.*
> *She's still **indignant** about not being invited.*
> *The politician was **infuriated** by the verbal attack.*
> ***Irate** callers jammed the phone lines to complain.*
> *I get **irritated** when he starts to whine.*
> *He forgot her birthday again and she's **livid**.*
> *The public was **outraged** when he was let out on parole.*

maddening, madding

Maddening describes something that makes one mad or is intensely irritating. The word **madding**, meaning "frenzied" or "acting madly", is used chiefly in the phrase *far from the **madding** crowd*, which is used to describe a secluded place (and is also the title of a novel by Thomas Hardy); to say *far from the **maddening** crowd* is to alter the original sense of the expression.

made, maid
The past tense of *make* is **made**. A female servant or young woman is a **maid**.

magnet, magnate
A substance that attracts metal is a **magnet**. A powerful business person is a **magnate**.

mail, male
The spelling is **mail** for the sending of letters or messages and for a type of armour. The opposite of *female* is **male**.

main, mane
The spelling is **main** in *the **main** reason* and *water **main***. The hair on a lion or horse is a **mane**.

main clause
M **G** (also **principal clause**) a clause in a complex sentence that could form a complete sentence by itself (compare SUBORDINATE CLAUSE).

male, mail
The opposite of *female* is **male**. The spelling is **mail** for the sending of letters or messages and for a type of armour.

mall, maul
A shopping centre is a **mall**. An animal which attacks someone **mauls** them.

man
Because the most common meaning of **man** is "a male human being", the use of the word to mean "any person" or "the human race", as in *All **men** are created equal* or ***man's** astounding technical achievements,* is often perceived as excluding women. To avoid accusations of sexism, it may be safest to use alternative constructions, e.g. *All people are created equal,* or *humankind's astounding technical achievements.*

mane, main
The hair on a lion or horse is a **mane**. The spelling is **main** in *the **main** reason* and *water **main***.

manikin, mannequin
An artist's model of a human body is a **manikin**. A model for displaying clothing is a **mannequin**.

mankind
Some people consider the use of **mankind** to mean "the human race" sexist; it might be safer to use **humankind** or **the human race**.

manner, manor
The spelling is **manner** for the way someone does something and in *to the **manner** born*. A large house is a **manor**.

manoeuvre
⚠ Warning: there is an *e* in the middle of **manoeuvre**.

M

mantel, mantle
The part shelf over a fireplace is a **mantel**. The spelling is **mantle** for a cloak or the region beneath the earth's crust.

marry, merry
To wed is to **marry**. The word meaning "joyous" is **merry**.

marshal, martial
The word pertaining to fighting is **martial**: ***martial** arts*. The spelling is **marshal** for an officer and to mean "arrange or draw up" and has only one *l*, except in the forms **marshalled** and **marshalling**.

marten, martin
The weasel-like mammal is a **marten**. The bird is a **martin**.

mask, masque

A covering for the face is a **mask**. A dramatic entertainment popular in Shakespeare's time was a **masque**.

mass noun

G a noun that is not countable and cannot be used with the indefinite article (*a*) or in the plural, e.g. *luggage, china, happiness*.

mauve

⚠ Warning: the pale purple colour is **mauve**.

may, can

Both **can** and **may** are used to express permission: *Can I go now? May I go now?* But because **can** is also used to indicate capability (*Can I sing?* = Am I able to sing?), in formal contexts **may** tends to be used to express permission (*May I sing?* = Am I allowed to sing?).

may, might

May and **might** can often be used interchangeably: most people see no difference in the sentences *It may rain* and *It might rain* (though according to some people **may** indicates a greater likelihood than **might** does). Note, however, the difference in the meanings of *A safety inspection might have averted disaster* (i.e. a disaster happened which could have been averted had there been a safety inspection), and *A safety inspection may have averted disaster* (i.e. no disaster took place, possibly because of a safety inspection). As well, use **might**, not **may**, after expressions like *If you'd been there* or *Had I known*, etc.: *If you'd been there you might have seen them; Had I known I might have been able to help.*

McIntosh, mackintosh

The apple is a **McIntosh**. A British term for a raincoat is **mackintosh**.

me, I

The use of **me** instead of **I** after the verb *to be*, as in *It's* **me** *again*, is now considered acceptable in writing as well as speech. In sentences like *It is **I** who knows you best*, however, **I** must be used instead of **me**. To avoid sounding excessively formal, such a sentence could be reworded *I'm the one who knows you best*, which is much more natural. See also THAN.

Never use **I** in sentences like *The teacher spoke to my father and I*, *The bus picked up my sister and I*, or *just between you and I*. In all these cases **I** should be replaced by **me**: *The teacher spoke to my father and **me**; The bus picked up my sister and **me**; just between you and **me***. To know whether to use **I** or **me**, determine which form would be appropriate if you were the only one mentioned: Just as you would say *The teacher spoke to **me*** (and not *The teacher spoke to I*), the correct form with *my father* is *The teacher spoke to **my father and me***. Similarly, because you would say *I went to see the teacher* (and not *Me went to see the teacher*), the correct form with *my father* is ***My father and I** went to see the teacher*.

M

meat, meet, mete

Animal flesh as food is **meat**. To come together with is to **meet**; the spelling is also **meet** in ***meet** the recommendations*. The spelling is **mete** in ***mete** out punishment*.

medal, meddle, metal, mettle

An award is a **medal**. To interfere is to **meddle**. Substances like steel, copper, and silver are **metals**. The spelling is **mettle** for "spirit" or "courage", as in "test your mettle".

media, medium

Media has traditionally been considered the plural of **medium**, as in *All the **media** were covering the story, including radio and TV*. Recently, however, **media** has come to be understood as a singular as well, referring to all media collectively, as in *The **media** always seems to be against us*. This usage is becoming well established, but because there are still many people who object to it, sticking with the plural might be the safest policy.

medieval

 Warning: remember the *i* in **medieval**.

meet, meat, mete

To come together with is to **meet**; the spelling is also **meet** in ***meet** the recommendations*. The food is spelled **meat**. The spelling is **mete** in ***mete** out punishment*.

memento

 Warning: **memento** does not begin with *moment-*.

(in) memoriam

Note that **in memoriam** ends in *-iam*, not *-ium*.

merengue, meringue

The dance is the **merengue**. The dessert is **meringue**.

merry, marry

The word meaning "joyous" is **merry**. To wed is to **marry**.

metal, mettle, medal

Substances like steel, copper, and silver are **metals**. The spelling is **mettle** for "spirit" or "courage", as in *test your **mettle***. An award is a **medal**.

meter, metre

A gauge or an instrument for measuring is a **meter**: *gas **meter**, parking **meter***. The unit of length is a **metre**; Canadians usually use **metre** for the rhythm in poetry.

mettle, metal, meddle

The spelling is **mettle** for "spirit" or "courage", as in *test* your **mettle**. Steel and copper are **metals**. To interfere is to **meddle**.

might, mite
Strength is **might**; **might** is also the spelling in *They said they **might** be late*. A small bug or thing is a **mite**.

might, may
May and **might** can often be used interchangeably: most people see no difference in the sentences *It **may** rain* and *It **might** rain* (though according to some people **may** indicates a greater likelihood than **might** does). Note, however, the difference in the meanings of *A safety inspection **might** have averted disaster* (i.e. a disaster happened which could have been averted had there been a safety inspection), and *A safety inspection **may** have averted disaster* (i.e. no disaster took place, possibly because of a safety inspection). As well, use **might**, not **may**, after expressions like *If you'd been there* or *Had I known*, etc.: *If you'd been there you **might** have seen them*; *Had I known I **might** have been able to help*.

might have
Note that in statements such as *It **might have** been even worse*, the correct expression is **might have** (or the contraction **might've**) and not "might of".

millennium
⚠ Warning: **millennium** is spelled with two *l*'s and two *n*'s.

miner, minor
Someone who works in a mine is a **miner**. Something of little importance is **minor**; a person who is underage is a **minor**.

minuscule
⚠ Warning: the first part of **minuscule** is *minus-*.

mischievous
Although the pronunciation "miss CHEE vee us" is very common, it is not considered standard by many people. The standard pronunciation is "MISS chiv us".

misdemeanour
Misdemeanour is not used officially in Canadian law, where the term **summary conviction offence** is used instead.

mislead, misled
Note that the past tense of **mislead** is **misled**: *I have never misled you and I will never mislead you.*

✗ mispell → misspell ✔
Warning: **misspell** is spelled with two *s*'s.

misplaced modifiers
In the sentence *As a single woman, he found her very interesting*, the phrase *as a single woman* should be modifying *her*, but its position in the sentence makes it sound like it is modifying *he*, which is silly. To guard against misplacing modifiers, try to keep them as close as possible to the person or thing they are modifying: *He found her interesting as a single woman.*

missal, missile
A book used by Catholics at Mass is a **missal**. A type of weapon is a **missile**.

misspell
⚠ Warning: remember to include both *s*'s in **misspell**.

mite, might
A small bug or thing is a **mite**. The word for strength is **might**; **might** is also the spelling in *They said they might be late.*

mixed metaphors

When using figurative language, try to avoid mixing incongruous metaphors, which may distract the reader or weaken serious writing with unintentional humour. Mixed metaphors usually occur when two or more figurative expressions that have become idiomatic are used together without considering the ludicrous image that is created by combining them: *He needs time to digest the nuts and bolts of the issue.* Consider the literal meaning of metaphors before using them together.

moccasin

⚠ Warning: there are two *c*'s and one *s* in **moccasin**.

modify

G (especially of an adjective or adverb) restrict or add to the meaning of another word or phrase: in *the playful kitten*, *playful* modifies *kitten*.

✗ momento → memento ✔
Warning: **memento** does not begin with *moment-*.

mood

G a form or set of forms of a verb serving to indicate whether it is to express a fact, command, wish, etc.: *subjunctive* **mood**.

moose, mousse

The animal is a **moose**. The whipped dessert or hair foam is **mousse**.

morn, mourn

A literary term for the morning is **morn**. To show sorrow is to **mourn**.

muscle, mussel

Body tissue is **muscle**. The shellfish is a **mussel**.

mute, moot

Something or someone that is silent is **mute**. An issue that is undecided or debatable or that is no longer of practical importance or relevance is **moot**: *The question of whether or not stores should be allowed to sell toy guns remains a **moot** point; The final score was 6-0, so whether or not the first goal should have counted is **moot**.*

myself

Do not misuse **myself**. Sentences like *Ivan, Marty, and myself went out to a movie* and *They were very kind to my wife and myself* are not recommended. It is better to say *Ivan, Marty, and I went out for dinner* and *They were very kind to my wife and me*. Reserve **myself** for reflexive uses like *I'll just help **myself** to a drink* or emphatic ones like *I **myself** was not offended, but Jerry and Angela were.*

naught, nought

The spelling is **naught** in *all for **naught*** and *come to **naught***. **Nought** is an archaic word for "nothing" and a British word for "zero".

nauseous

It is perfectly fine to use **nauseous** to mean "queasy", as in *The smell made me **nauseous***. Some people argue that it can only mean "causing nausea", as in *The **nauseous** smell made me queasy*, but the first sense is by far the most common even in edited writing.

naval, navel

The word pertaining to fighting ships is **naval**. The belly button is the **navel**.

nave, knave

The largest part of a church is the **nave**. A scoundrel is a **knave**.

navel, naval

The belly button is the **navel**. The word pertaining to fighting ships is **naval**.

need, knead

To require is to **need**. To work dough or clay is to **knead** it.

Negro

Avoid using **Negro**; use **black** instead.

neither

Although **neither** is often treated as a plural in informal spoken English, as in **Neither** *of them are very good*, in careful writing it is better to use singular verbs in such cases: **Neither** *of them is very good*. When using the construction, **neither... nor...**, the verb can be either singular or plural, though if either subject is plural the verb tends to be plural: **Neither** *he* **nor** *she has been there*; **Neither** *he* **nor** *his sisters have been there*.

nerve-racking

Note that there is no *w* before the *r* in **nerve-racking**.

next door, next-door

Note the difference in spelling between *the boy* **next door** and *the* **next-door** *neighbour*. There is a hyphen when the latter kind of structure is used.

nice, very nice

Instead of saying that something is **nice** or **very nice**, try to use more precise and interesting adjectives to describe things:

> We had a **delightful/splendid/enjoyable** time
> a **satisfying/delicious/exquisite** meal
> a **fashionable/stylish/elegant/chic** outfit
> This is a **cozy/comfortable/attractive** room

*She is **kind/friendly/likeable/amiable***
*Our adviser is **compassionate/understanding/***
  sympathetic
*a **thoughtful/considerate/caring** gesture*
When describing the weather, you can use words like
pleasant, ***fair***, ***mild***, and ***fine*** instead of ***nice***.

night, knight
The opposite of *day* is **night**. The spelling is **knight** for
the medieval soldier and the chess piece.

nit, knit
The eggs of lice are **nits**; a fussy person is a **nitpicker**.
The spelling is **knit** for working with yarn and in ***knit***
***one's** brow*.

nohow, know-how
The word **nohow**, meaning "by no means", is not used
in standard English. **Know-how**, referring to knowledge
or skill, is perfectly fine.

non-defining clause
G (also **non-restrictive clause**) a clause which gives
information about the antecedent merely to describe it,
not to give information essential to identifying it. In *The*
books, which are on the table, used to belong to Anna, the
clause *which are on the table* is a non-defining clause
because it gives some more information about the books
but is not essential to identify *which* books out of all the
books in the world used to belong to Anna. Non-defining
clauses must be set off by commas, and cannot be
introduced by *that*.

none
Despite claims that **none** must always be followed by a
singular verb, the verb may in fact be either singular or
plural: ***None** of my friends was more upset than Isabel; I*
*looked for my friends, but **none** of them were at the party.*

not, naught, knot
The spelling is **naught** in *all for **naught*** and *come to **naught***. Something tied or tangled, a unit of speed, and a growth on a tree are all **knots**.

nought, naught
Nought is an archaic word for "nothing" and a British word for "zero" The spelling is **naught** in *all for **naught*** and *come to **naught***.

noun
G a word (other than a pronoun) or group of words used to name or identify any of a class of persons, places, or things (COMMON NOUN), or a particular one of these (PROPER NOUN).

number
the form of a word showing whether one or more than ·
G one person or thing is being talked about: *girl* is singular in number, while *girls* is plural in number.

a number of/the number of
Use a plural verb after **a number of**, e.g. *A **number of** people were seen* (not *was seen*). Use a singular verb after **the number of**, e.g. *The **number of** shootings is alarming* (not *are alarming*).

nuptial
⚠ Warning: the word **nuptial**, designating things relating to marriage or weddings, ends in -*tial*, not -*tual*.

oar, ore
Rowers use **oars**. Rocks from which minerals are extracted are **ore**.

object
G a noun, pronoun, or noun phrase that refers to a person or thing that is affected by the action of a verb (called the DIRECT OBJECT), e.g. *She likes **us**; that the action is done to*

or for (called the INDIRECT OBJECT), e.g. *She gave **us** a call;* or that is governed by a preposition, e.g. *She's with **us**.*

occur, occurrence

⚠ Warning: **occurring**, **occurred**, and **occurrence** are all spelled with two *c*'s and two *r*'s.

✗ Octoberfest → Oktoberfest ✔

Warning: the annual festival is spelled **Oktoberfest**.

of, have

Use **have**, not **of**, in expressions like **might have**, **could have**, **would have**, and **should have**: *I **should have** been more careful* (not *I should of been more careful*).

off, off of

In careful writing avoid using **off of** when **off** by itself would do, as in *The plate fell off of the table*, which would be better written as *The plate fell **off** the table*.

off

Although sentences like *I bought the guitar **off** my neighbour* are common, this construction is best avoided in formal writing and speech. It is better to say *I bought the guitar from my neighbour*.

⚠ Oktoberfest

Warning: the annual festival is spelled with a *k*: **Oktoberfest**.

omit, omission

Note that there is only one *m* in **omit** and **omission**.

on-board, on board

Note the difference in spelling between ***on-board*** *equipment* and *the equipment is **on board***. There is no hyphen when the latter kind of structure is used.

one

When you're using **one** as a pronoun, as in *One should always be careful*, and you have to refer back to **one** later on in a sentence, it is best to repeat the word **one**, as in *One should always be careful not to offend one's friends*, rather than use *his, her, his or her*, or *their*. However, too many **one**'s in a sentence, as in *One should always take **one's** time doing **one's** homework*, may sound overly formal or even clumsy; in such cases use **you** instead: *You should always take your time doing your homework*. Be careful, though, not to use **you** in formal essays: do not write *When **you** read this novel, **you** feel a lot of empathy for the main character*. Use **one** or *the reader*.

only

In normal speech it is standard to place **only** just before the verb, as in *I **only** wanted to talk to you*. In careful writing, however, you should consider placing **only** where it is least ambiguous. Consider the possible meanings of *The loon can **only** be heard in the morning mist.*: It can mean that *the morning mist* is the only place the loon can be heard, or that the loon can be *heard* there but not seen; if the first sense was intended, the sentence could have been written less ambiguously as *Only in the morning mist can the loon be heard*.

ophthalmology, ophthalmologist

⚠ Warning: do not forget the *h* after the *p* and the *l* before the *m* in **ophthalmology** and related words.

oral, aural

The word pertaining to speaking or the mouth is **oral**. The word pertaining to hearing or the ear is **aural**.

ore, oar

Minerals are extracted from **ore**. A boat is propelled with **oars**.

ours

Note that there is no apostrophe in **ours**: *Don't touch it—it's **ours***.

ourself, ourselves

Do not use **ourself**; use **ourselves** instead.

ourselves

Do not misuse **ourselves**. Sentences like *The players and ourselves have reached a deal* and *They offered the committee and ourselves a chance to vote* are not recommended. It is better to say *We and the players have reached a deal* and *They offered the committee and us a chance to vote*. Reserve **ourselves** for reflexive uses like *We helped **ourselves** to ice cream* or emphatic ones like *We **ourselves** are in no position to judge their crimes*.

out-of-work, out of work

Note the difference in spelling between ***out-of-work*** actors and *thousands of people were **out of work***. There is no hyphen when the latter kind of structure is used.

outside, outside of

The use of **outside of** in sentences like *They live **outside of** Pembroke* is perfectly acceptable in standard English, though some people prefer constructions without the *of*, e.g. *They live **outside** Pembroke*.

over-the-counter, over the counter

Note the difference in spelling between *an **over-the-counter** drug* and *this medication is available **over the counter***. There is no hyphen when the latter kind of structure is used.

pail, pale

A bucket is a **pail**. The spelling is **pale** for something lacking colour or weak, and in *beyond the **pale***.

pain, pane
Something that hurts is a **pain**. A sheet of glass is a **pane**.

pair, pear, pare
The spelling is **pair** for a set of two and in *au pair*. The fruit is a **pear**. To trim is to **pare**.

palate, palette, pallet
The roof of the mouth or the sense of taste is the **palate**. A board for mixing paint is a **palette**. The spelling is **pallet** for a bed and for a shipping skid.

pale, pail
The spelling is **pale** for something lacking colour or weak, and in *beyond the pale*. A bucket is a **pail**.

palette, palate, pallet
A board for mixing paint is a **palette**. The roof of the mouth or the sense of taste is the **palate**. The spelling is **pallet** for a bed and for a shipping skid.

pane, pain
A sheet of glass is a **pane**. Something that hurts is a **pain**.

P

parallel
Note that in **parallel** the first *l* is doubled but the *r* and the second *l* are not.

parallel structure
Parallel structure refers to sentence structure in which related parts have the same grammatical function, e.g. all nouns, all adjectives, etc. The failure to use parallel structure makes writing awkward and potentially unclear. For example, the sentence *As a result of abuse, children may become withdrawn, too eager to please, aggressive, demanding, or have suicidal tendencies* is much less awkward if it is rewritten as *As a result of abuse, children may become withdrawn, fawning, aggressive, demanding, or suicidal.*

paraphernalia

Warning: do not forget the *r* immediately before the *n* in **paraphernalia**. Although traditionally a plural noun, **paraphernalia** can also be treated as a singular.

pare, pair, pear

To trim is to **pare**. The spelling is **pair** for a set of two and in **au pair**. The fruit is a **pear**.

parentheses

For guidance on the use of parentheses see Appendix 1.

parish, perish

A church district is a **parish**. To die is to **perish**.

parliament

⚠ Warning: do not forget the *i* after the *l* in **parliament**.

participial

G involving a participle; for example, the word *cutting* in *a cutting remark* is a **participial adjective**, because *cutting* is the present participle of the verb *to cut*.

participial phrase

G a phrase starting with a participle, e.g. "*Rounding a bend*, they suddenly saw the ocean", or "I am reading an article *discussing free trade*". When using participial phrases, be especially careful to avoid a DANGLING PARTICIPLE.

participle

G a word formed from a verb, e.g. *going, gone, being, been*, and used in compound verb forms, e.g. *is going, has been*, or as an adjective, e.g. *working poor, burnt toast*, or to introduce a participial phrase, e.g. *going down the road*.

passed, past

The past tense of the verb *pass* is **passed**: *I **passed** him in* *the hall*. Do not confuse this with the preposition **past**, as in *I walked **past** him in the hall*.

passive

G (also **passive voice**) the form of a verb used when the subject is affected by the action of the verb, as in *They were killed*. Often it is better to use the active voice when writing than the passive voice; *I sent the letter* is more effective than *The letter was sent by me*.

pasteurized

Do not forget the *e* before the *u* in **pasteurized**.

pastime

⚠ Warning: **pastime** is spelled with only one *s*.

peak, peek, pique

A highest point is a **peak**. A quick look is a **peek**. The spelling is **pique** in *It **piqued** my interest* and *He stormed off in a fit of **pique***.

peal, peel

The spelling is **peal** in ***peals** of laughter*, ***peals** of thunder*, and *the **peal** of the bells*. The skin of a fruit is its **peel**.

pear, pair, pare

The fruit is a **pear**. A set of two is a **pair**. To trim is to **pare**.

pearl, purl

A white gem taken from oysters is a **pearl**. A type of knitting stitch is a **purl**.

pedal, peddle, petal

A foot-operated lever is a **pedal**, and you **pedal** your bicycle and **soft-pedal** an issue. To sell or promote is to **peddle**. Flowers have **petals**.

peddler, pedlar
Both **peddler** and **pedlar** are acceptable for a travelling seller of small items.

peek, peak, pique
A quick look is a **peek**. A highest point is a **peak**. The spelling is *pique* in *It piqued my interest* and *He stormed off in a fit of pique*.

peel, peal
The skin of a fruit is its **peel**. The spelling is **peal** in *peals of laughter*, *peals of thunder*, and the *peal of the bells*.

pejorative
⚠ Warning: There is no *r* before the *j* in **pejorative**, a word used as a put-down.

penultimate
Penultimate does not mean "absolutely ultimate" or "not surpassable". It means "second-last": *The penultimate chapter needs revision*.

period
For guidance in the use of the period see Appendix 1.

perish, parish
To die is to **perish**. A church district is a **parish**.

✗ perjorative → pejorative ✔
Warning: There is no *r* before the *j* in **pejorative**, a word used as a put-down.

✗ perogative → prerogative ✔
Warning: **prerogative** begins *pre-*, not *per-*.

✗ perscription → prescription ✔
Warning: a **prescription** for medicine begins *pre-*, not *per-*.

persevere
⚠ Warning: there is no *r* immediately before the *v* in **persevere**.

person
G a category used in the classification of pronouns, verb forms, etc., according to whether they indicate the speaker (**first person**: *I, we*), the addressee (**second person**: *you*), or a third party (**third person**: *he, she, it, one, they*).

personal pronoun
each of the pronouns *I, you, he, she, it, we, they, me, him,* **G** *her, us, them.*

personnel
Note that there are two *n*'s in **personnel**.

persue → pursue ✔
✗ Warning: **pursue** is spelled with two *u*'s.

peruse
Peruse has two nearly opposite meanings. Its traditional sense is "to examine thoroughly or in detail", as in *The editor perused the article to find every mistake.* The more recent sense is "to skim quickly", as in *I only had time to peruse the newspaper before leaving for work.* Readers should be aware that **peruse** may be used in either of these senses, and it is best avoided when the context does not make the meaning clear.

perverbial → proverbial ✔
✗ Warning: the first three letters of **proverbial**, as in *the* **proverbial** *cloud with a silver lining* are *pro*, not *per*; **proverbial** is derived from the word *proverb*.

petal, pedal
Flowers have **petals**. A foot-operated lever is a **pedal**.

phase, faze

Each stage of a process is a **phase**; to introduce something gradually is to **phase** it in. If something doesn't bother you, it doesn't **faze** you.

phenomenon, phenomena

Phenomena is a plural noun: *These **phenomena** are not fully understood.* It should not be used as a singular. The singular of **phenomena** is **phenomenon**: *this warmth that greened the valley was not so much a season as a brief **phenomenon**.*

Philippine, Filipina/Filipino, Pilipino

A person from the Philippines is a **Filipina** or a **Filipino**; the language of the Philippines is **Pilipino**.

phrasal verb

G   an idiomatic phrase consisting of a verb and an adverb, e.g. *break down*, or a verb and a preposition, e.g. *see to*.

phrase

G   a group of words lacking a subject and/or predicate but functioning as part of a sentence.

pidgin, pigeon

A type of language is a **pidgin**. A small city bird is a **pigeon**.

pitcher, picture

A jug or a baseball player is a **pitcher**. A painting or photograph is a **picture**.

plain, plane

The spelling is **plain** for something simple or ordinary and for a prairie. The spelling is **plane** for an airplane, a flat surface, and a woodworking device.

Plasticine, Pleistocene

The proprietary name for a type of modelling substance is **Plasticine**. The first epoch of the Quaternary period is the **Pleistocene** epoch.

playwright, playwriting

A person who writes plays is a **playwright**. The writing of plays is **playwriting**.

plum, plumb

The fruit is a **plum**. The spelling is **plumb** in *plumb line*, *plumb the depths of*, and *plumb tuckered out*.

plus

Do not use **plus** as a conjunction, as in sentences like *We saw clowns, plus there were lions and elephants*. Such usage is not standard. An acceptable alternative might be *We saw clowns, and there were lions and elephants too*.

poinsettia

⚠ Warning: **poinsettia** ends in -*settia*, not -*setta*, and begins with *poin*-, not *point*-.

point, pointe

The tip of something sharp is a **point**. Ballerinas dance on **pointe** in **pointe** shoes.

pole, poll

The spelling is **pole** for a post and in *North **Pole*** and ***pole** position*; a person from Poland is a **Pole**. A vote or survey is a **poll**; a tax on every adult is a **poll** tax.

polka, polka dot

⚠ Warning: both the dance called the **polka** and **polka dots** are spelled with an *l*.

populous, populace
A city with many people is **populous**. The people living in an area are the **populace**.

pore, pour
A tiny opening in the skin is a **pore**; if you read something intently, you **pore** over it. To dispense liquid is to **pour**.

possess
Note that there are two double-*s*'s in **possess**.

possessive adjective
G each of the adjectives indicating possession: *my, your, her, his, its, our, their*.

possessive pronoun
G each of the pronouns indicating possession: *mine, yours, hers, his, its, ours, theirs*. Note that no apostrophes are used in possessive pronouns.

pour, pore
To dispense liquid is to **pour**. A tiny opening in the skin is a **pore**; if you read something intently, you **pore** over it.

practice, practise
In Canada the noun is always spelled with a *c* (**practice**) and the verb usually with an *s* (**practise**): *I'm late for soccer **practice**; I have to **practise** some more on the piano.*

Prairie, prairie
When referring to Alberta, Saskatchewan, and Manitoba, capitalize **Prairie**: *the **Prairie** provinces, the **Prairies***. When referring to flat grassland, do not capitalize **prairie**: *prairie wildlife*.

pray, prey
To say prayers is to **pray**; the insect is a **praying**

mantis. A hunter's victim is its **prey**; if you take advantage of someone you **prey** upon them; if something bothers you it **preys** on your mind.

precede, proceed
To come or go before is to **precede**: *April precedes May.*
To move forwards or to continue is to **proceed**: *Please proceed to the next level.*

predicate
G a part of a sentence containing a verb that makes a statement about the subject of the verb, e.g. *went home* in *Earl went home.*

prejudice
Note that there is no *d* before the *j* in **prejudice**.

prejudice, prejudiced
Note that the adjective is **prejudiced**: *prejudiced attitudes.*

premier, premiere
The head of a province is a **premier**; the spelling is **premier** in *Canada's premier theatre company.* The first performance of something is a **premiere**.

P

pre-nuptial
⚠ Warning: the word **pre-nuptial**, as in *a pre-nuptial agreement*, ends in -tial, not -tual.

preposition
G a word or group of words, such as *in, from, to, out of,* and *on behalf of,* used before a noun or pronoun to show place, position, time, or method: *the man on the platform, came after dinner, what did you do it for?*. There is a traditional view that it is incorrect to put a preposition at the end of a sentence, as in *Where do you come from* or *She's not a writer I've ever come across.* This "rule" was

formed on the basis that, since in Latin a preposition cannot come after the word it governs or is linked with, the same should be true of English. The problem is that English is not like Latin in this respect, and in many cases (particularly in questions and with phrasal verbs) the attempt to move the preposition produces awkward, unnatural-sounding results. In standard English the placing of a preposition at the end of a sentence is widely accepted, provided that the use sounds natural and the meaning is clear.

prepositional phrase
G a phrase formed with a preposition, e.g. *on the hill*.

prerogative
⚠ Warning: **prerogative** begins *pre-*, not *per-*.

prescribe, proscribe
A doctor **prescribes** medicine. If something is **proscribed**, it is forbidden.

prescription
P ⚠ Warning: a **prescription** for medicine begins *pre-*, not *per-*.

pretension
⚠ Warning: **pretension** ends in *-sion*, not *-tion*.

prey, pray
A hunter's victim is its **prey**; if you take advantage of someone you **prey** upon them; if something bothers you it **preys** on your mind. To say prayers is to **pray**; the insect is a **praying mantis**.

principal, principle
The spelling is **principal** for the head of a school, in *the principal reason*, and for an amount of money lent or invested. A fundamental truth or law is a **principle**: *Distracting your opponent is against the **principles** of fair*

play; **principle** is also the spelling in *I support the idea in principle* and in *they refused on **principle***.

principal clause

G See MAIN CLAUSE.

pristine

Using **pristine** to mean "unspoiled" is now perfectly standard; using it to mean "clean like new", as in *After two hours of careful washing, the car was **pristine***, is also acceptable, though the occasional objection to it is still heard.

privilege

⚠ Warning: there is no *d* before the *g* in **privilege**; do not forget the *i* before the *l*.

proceed, precede

To move forwards or to continue is to **proceed**: *Please **proceed** to the next level*. To come or go before is to **precede**: *April **precedes** May*.

profit, prophet

The money made by a company is a **profit**. A person who foretells is a **prophet**.

P

pronoun

G a word used instead of and to indicate a noun already mentioned or known, especially to avoid repetition, e.g. *we, theirs, this, ourselves*.

pronunciation

⚠ Warning: there is no *o* in the second syllable of **pronunciation**. Although the word is often pronounced, by analogy with *pronounce*, as if the second syllable rhymed with *bounce*, this is not correct in standard English. The standard pronunciation has the second syllable rhyming with *dunce*.

proper noun

G (also **proper name**) a word that is the name of a person, a place, an institution, etc., and is written with a capital letter, for example *Tom, Mrs. Jones, Rome, Canada, the St. Lawrence River.*

prophecy, prophesy

An inspired prediction is a **prophecy**, which is pronounced "PROFFA see". To make such a prediction is to **prophesy**, pronounced "PROFFA sigh".

prophet, profit

A person who foretells is a **prophet**. The money made by a company is a **profit**.

proscribe, prescribe

If something is **proscribed**, it is forbidden. A doctor **prescribes** medicine.

proscription, prescription

An act of forbidding is a **proscription**. A doctor's note authorizing medication is a **prescription**.

P

prostrate, prostate

Someone lying face downwards is **prostrate**. The gland in men's bodies is the **prostate**.

protest, protest against

In Canada it is perfectly acceptable to use either *We **protested against** their decision* or *We **protested** their decision,* despite the claims by some that the first use is redundant and by others that the second use is ungrammatical.

⚠ **proverbial**

Warning: the first three letters of **proverbial**, as in *the **proverbial** cloud with a silver lining,* are *pro,* not *per;* **proverbial** is derived from the word *proverb.*

publicly
Note that **publicly** ends in *-ly*, not in *-ally*.

pursue
⚠ Warning: **pursue** is spelled with two *u*'s.

puss, pus
A cat is a **puss**. Liquid matter from bodily infections is **pus**.

put, putt
To move something somewhere is to **put** it there. The golf stroke is a **putt**.

quadriplegic
⚠ Warning: the first part of **quadriplegic** is *quadri-*, not *quadra-*.

qualifier
G a word, especially an adjective or adverb, that describes another word in a particular way: in *the open door*, *open* is a qualifier, describing the door.

quandary
⚠ Warning: **quandary** is spelled with two *a*'s.

question mark
For guidance on the use of the question mark see Appendix 1.

quick, quickly
The use of **quick** as an adverb is usually restricted to set phrases, such as *Come **quick**, **Quick**—do something!*, and *Get rich **quick***. Outside of such expressions, the adverb **quickly** is more standard: *We ran **quickly***, not *We ran **quick***.

quotation marks
For guidance on the use of quotation marks see Appendix 1.

rack, wrack

The spelling is always **rack** in *storage* **rack** and **rack** *of lamb*; Canadians also prefer **rack** over **wrack** in **rack** *up points*, **rack** *your brains*, **rack** *and ruin*, and *nerve-***racking**. **Wrack** is a type of seaweed or a wreck.

racket, racquet

The spelling is **racket** in *stop making such a* **racket** and *they got involved in some* **racket** *and ended up in jail*. **Racquet** is the usual Canadian spelling in *tennis* **racquet**.

rain, rein, reign

Water falling from the sky is **rain**. The horse strap is a **rein**, which is also the spelling used in **rein** *something in*. A Queen who is ruling is **reigning**; Canadian Confederation happened during the **reign** of Queen Victoria.

raise, raze

To lift higher is to **raise**. To destroy something completely or tear something down is to **raze** it.

rancour, rancorous

Note that Canadians normally put a *u* in **rancour**, but always remove that *u* from **rancorous**.

R

rapt, wrapped

To be fully absorbed in something or carried away with feeling or thought is to be **rapt**. To be enveloped is to be **wrapped**.

ravage, ravish

Do not confuse **ravage** and **ravish**. To **ravage** is to devastate or plunder. To **ravish** is to enrapture or to rape.

re-

Re- is normally written with a hyphen when the word to which it is attached begins with *e*, as in *re-enact*, or to distinguish the compound from a one-word form, e.g. *re-form* ("form again"), which is distinguished from *reform* ("change").

read, reed
To understand written words is to **read**. The stalk of a plant or the part of a musical instrument mouthpiece is a **reed**.

real, really
The use of **real** instead of **really** as an adverb, as in *I'm real hungry*, is considered non-standard and should not be used in writing.

real, reel
Something authentic is **real**. A winding device or spool is a **reel**; a **reel** is also a dance and music, and is used in *sent them reeling*.

reason
The well-established idioms in **the reason why** *I was late* and **the reason is because** *my car broke down* continue to be strongly criticized as redundant by many teachers of composition. To avoid such criticism, you should use constructions like **the reason** *I was late* and **the reason is that** *my car broke down*.

R

✗ reccommend → recommend ✔
Warning: double the *m* but not the *c* in **recommend**.

receive
⚠ Warning: the second *e* comes before the *i* in **receive**.

reconnaissance
Remember to double both the *n* and the *s* in **reconnaissance**.

recurrence, recurrent
Note that there are two *r*'s in **recurrence** and **recurrent**.

reed, read
The stalk of a plant or the part of a musical instrument mouthpiece is a **reed**. To understand written words is to **read**.

reel, real
A winding device or spool is a **reel**; a **reel** is also a dance and music, and is used in *sent them **reeling***. Something authentic is **real**.

reflexive
G **1** (of a word or form) referring back to the subject of a sentence (especially of a pronoun, e.g. *myself*). **2** (of a verb) having a reflexive pronoun as its object (as in *to wash oneself*).

reflexive pronoun
G each of the pronouns referring back to the subject of a clause: *myself, yourself, himself, herself, itself, oneself, ourselves, yourselves, themselves*. Note that there is no reflexive pronoun *theirselves*.

reign, rein
A Queen who is ruling is **reigning**; Canadian Confederation happened during the **reign** of Queen Victoria. The horse strap is a **rein**, which is also the spelling used in ***rein** something in* and *give a free **rein** to*.

✗ **reknown, reknowned** → **renown, renowned** **✔**
Warning: there is no *k* in **renown** or **renowned**. It is important not to confuse these words: **renown** is a noun meaning "fame", while **renowned** is an adjective meaning "famous". Note the difference between *She is a writer of great **renown*** and *She is a **renowned** writer*.

relative clause
G a clause attached to an antecedent by a relative pronoun, e.g. *who screamed* in *the man who screamed*.

R

relative pronoun

G a pronoun referring to an expressed or implied antecedent and attaching a subordinate clause to it, e.g. *who* in *the man who screamed*; other relative pronouns are *whom*, *which*, and *that*.

remuneration

⚠ Warning: the second syllable of **remuneration** (payment or a reward) is -*mun*-, not -*num*-.

renown, renowned

⚠ Warning: there is no *k* in **renown** or **renowned**. It is important not to confuse these words: **renown** is a noun meaning "fame", while **renowned** is an adjective meaning "famous". Note the difference between *She is a writer of great **renown*** and *She is a **renowned** writer*.

reseed, recede

To sow seeds again is to **reseed**. To move back gradually from a previous position is to **recede**: *The flood waters have begun to **recede***; *a **receding** hairline*.

rest, wrest

To relax and recover strength is to **rest**. If you take something forcibly from someone's possession, you **wrest** it from them.

R

restaurateur, restauranteur

The word spelled with an *n*, **restauranteur**, is becoming increasingly common, but there are still many people who consider it incorrect.

restrictive

G (of a clause or phrase) specifying which particular thing or things are being discussed, as opposed to merely describing them; in *The books which are on the table used to belong to Anna*, the clause *which are on the table* is restrictive because it tells us *which* books used to belong to

Anna, but if we insert commas around the clause, *The books, which are on the table, used to belong to Anna,* it merely tells us where the books are and is therefore not restrictive. Restrictive clauses are also called DEFINING CLAUSES.

retch, wretch
To gag is to **retch**. An unfortunate or wicked person is a **wretch**.

review, revue
A critical assessment is a **review**. A theatrical entertainment is a **revue**.

rhythm
⚠ Warning: there are two *h*'s in **rhythm**.

right, rite, write, wright
The opposite of *left* is **right**; something just or correct is **right**; **right** is also the spelling in *right* away and *right* angle. A religious observance is a **rite**. To put words on paper is to **write**. The maker of something is a **wright**.

ring, wring
The spelling is **ring** for the sound of a bell and the band worn on the finger. If you extract something by pressure, you **wring** it; you can **wring** clothes, someone's hand, or a chicken's neck; you can also **wring** someone's heart or concessions from someone.

ringer, wringer
Two people who look very much alike are **dead ringers**. The spelling is **wringer** in *put through the wringer*.

rite, right, write, wright
A religious observance is a **rite**. The opposite of *left* is **right**; something just or correct is **right**; **right** is also the spelling in *right* away and *right* angle. To put words

on paper is to **write**. The maker of something is a
wright.

root, route
The spelling is **root** for the underground part of a plant, in
the phrase ***root*** *out,* and for the verb meaning "to support
with cheering". The path you follow to reach a destination
is a **route**, which is also the spelling in *paper* **route**.

rot, wrought
To decay is to **rot**. Black iron used to make decorative
fences and gates is **wrought** iron.

rout, route
An overwhelming defeat is a **rout**; to cut a groove in
wood is to **rout**. The path you follow to reach a
destination is a **route**, which is also the spelling in *paper*
route.

row, roe
A line of things is a **row**; to propel a boat with oars is to
row. Fish eggs are **roe**; a **roe** is also a type of deer.

ruff, rough
A frill worn around the neck is a **ruff**. The opposite of
smooth is **rough**.

✗ rythm → rhythm ✔
Warning: there are two *h*'s in **rhythm**.

S

sacrilegious
⚠ Warning: the word **sacrilegious** does not come from the
word **religious**. The middle part is *-rileg-*, not *-relig-*.

sad, very sad
Instead of saying that someone or something is **sad** or
very sad, try to use more precise and interesting
adjectives such as the following:

> *unhappy/upsetting/distressing* news
> a *tragic/heartbreaking/poignant* tale
> I was *miserable/despondent/disconsolate/
> heartbroken* when she left
> a *gloomy/depressed/melancholy* mood
> a *dejected/downhearted/downcast/woebegone*
> expression
> The event was *unfortunate/deplorable/lamentable/
> regrettable*
> a *sorry/pathetic/wretched* state of affairs
> Our hockey team is pretty *pitiful/dreadful/feeble*

sail, sale

The wind-catching sheet on a boat is a **sail**. Something being sold is for **sale**.

✗ sargent → sergeant ✔

Warning: **sergeant** (a military or police officer) begins with *ser-*, not *sar-*.

sashay, sachet

To move casually is to **sashay**. A small packet of perfume or seasonings is a **sachet**.

scull, skull

An oar or small rowboat is a **scull**; a fish migration is a **scull**. The head of a skeleton is the **skull**.

seam, seem

Two pieces of cloth are joined at a **seam**. To appear to be is to **seem**.

secede, succeed

A country or nation that officially leaves an alliance or federal union in order to become independent is said to **secede**: *In 1860, South Carolina became the first state to secede from the United States.* When somebody becomes the rightful holder of a title or position, they **succeed** the person who formerly held the title or they **succeed to** the position itself: *Jamal succeeded Tracey as budget chief; Elizabeth succeeded to the throne in 1558.*

secession, succession
The withdrawal of a country or nation from an alliance or federal union in order to become independent is **secession**: *Demonstrators at a rally in Montreal urged Quebecers to vote against secession.* The process in which a person takes over an official position or title is **succession**: *She's third in order of succession to the throne.*

seem, seam
To appear to be is to **seem**. Two pieces of cloth are joined at a **seam**.

seize
⚠ Warning: **seize** is an exception to the "*i* before *e* except after *c*" rule. In **seize** the *e* comes before the *i*.

seller, cellar
Someone who sells is a **seller**. A basement is a **cellar**; a container for holding salt is a **saltcellar**.

semicolon
For guidance in the use of the semicolon see Appendix 1.

sensor, censer, censor, censure,
A device that detects light or motion is a **sensor**. A vessel for burning incense is a **censer**. To remove something objectionable from a book or movie is to **censor** it; a person who removes such matter is a **censor**. To criticize something harshly is to **censure** it.

sensual, sensuous
Both **sensual** and **sensuous** are normally used to refer to pleasures of the senses, and nowadays both usually suggest sexuality. Traditionally, **sensuous** has been the

more neutral term, used to describe the pleasures that music and other arts give to the senses, but today there seems to be little distinction made between the words.

sent, cent, scent
The past tense of *to send* is **sent**. A penny is a **cent**. A smell is a **scent**.

sentence
G   a set of words expressing a statement, a question, or an order, usually containing a subject and a verb.

sentence fragment
G   a writing error where a dependent clause or a phrase is treated as if it were a complete sentence, separated from the independent clause to which it belongs by a period. Examples of sentence fragments are the following:

> I didn't see the film. *Because I felt that it would be too violent for my taste.*
> It was a hilarious moment. *One that I shall never forget.*
> He gave me half his sandwich. *Being of a generous nature.*

separate
⚠ Warning: **separate** is spelled with an *a* before the *r*.

serf, surf
A feudal labourer, e.g. in the Middle Ages, is a **serf**. To ride the waves at a beach is to **surf**; **surf** is also the spelling in *surfing* the Net.

sergeant
⚠ Warning: **sergeant** (a military or police officer) begins with *ser-*, not *sar-*.

serial, cereal
Something produced in series or in instalments is **serial**;

serial is also the spelling in **serial** killer. Grain or breakfast food is **cereal**.

sew, sow
To work with needle and thread is to **sew**. To plant seeds in a field is to **sow**.

shaky
⚠ Warning: **shaky**, meaning "unsteady" or "unreliable", does not end in -ey.

shear, sheer
When you cut or trim something you **shear** it: **shear** a hedge; **shear** a sheep's wool; large scissors are **shears**. Something very steep is **sheer**; thin curtains are **sheers**; **sheer** is also used to mean "absolute", as in **sheer** luck or **sheer** genius.

sherbet
⚠ Warning: there is no r immediately before the t in **sherbet**.

shook, shaken
Note that while it's common to hear They were **shook** up after the accident, the standard past participle of shake is **shaken**: The accident left them **shaken**.

shoo-in
⚠ Warning: something sure to succeed is a **shoo-in**, not a shoe-in.

S

shoot, chute
To fire a weapon is to **shoot**. A channel, rapid, or parachute is a **chute**; garbage is sent down a **chute**.

should have
In statements such as You **should have** been better prepared, the correct expression is **should have** (or the contraction **should've**) and not should of.

✗ sieze → seize ✔

Warning: **seize** is an exception to the "*i* before *e* except after *c*" rule. In **seize** the *e* comes before the *i*.

sight, site

The ability to see is **sight**; the noteworthy features of an area are its **sights**: *We're going to Montreal to see the sights*. A place where something is situated is a **site**; an Internet location is a **website**.

signet, cygnet

A small seal set in a ring is a **signet**. A young swan is a **cygnet**.

silicon, silicone

The element used in electronic components is **silicon**. The soft compound used in caulking, implants, etc. is **silicone**.

silhouette

⚠ Warning: **silhouette** is spelled with an *h* immediately after the *l*.

sing, sung, sang

Do not use **sung** for the past tense of **sing**, as in *She sung three songs* (the correct past tense is **sang**). **Sung** is only used as a past participle, as in *The song she had **sung** the evening before was still playing in their heads*.

sink, sunk, sank, sunken

While it is not wrong to use **sunk** as the past tense of **sink**, as in *Our spirits **sunk** when we heard the news*, **sank** is by far more common in Canadian speech and writing and sounds much less informal. Note that the past participle is **sunk**, not **sunken**, which is used only as an adjective: *The ship had **sunk** more than three hundred years earlier, but the divers were still hoping to find **sunken** treasure*.

S

site, sight
A place where something is situated is a **site**; an Internet location is a **website**. The ability to see is **sight**; the noteworthy features of an area are its **sights**: *We're going to Montreal to see the sights*.

skull, scull
The head of a skeleton is the **skull**. An oar or small rowboat is a **scull**; a fish migration is a **scull**.

slay, sleigh
To kill is to **slay**. A large sled is a **sleigh**.

slight, sleight
Something small is **slight**. Magicians perform tricks using *sleight of hand*.

slow, slowly
The use of **slow** as an adverb instead of **slowly** is standard in compounds such as ***slow**-acting*, ***slow**-burning*; it is also established in short imperative expressions such as *go **slow***. In sentences such as *He drives too **slow*** and *Go as **slow** as you can*, however, **slowly** would be preferable, especially in formal contexts.

smoky, smokey
The spelling is usually **smoky** for something related to smoke. **Smokey** is a nickname for a highway police officer.

S

smooth, smoothly
⚠ Warning: the verb **to smooth** is not spelled with an *e* at the end. The use of **smooth** as an adverb is usually restricted to set phrases such as *goes down **smooth***. Outside of such expressions, the adverb **smoothly** is more standard: write *The engine runs **smoothly***, not *The engine runs **smooth***.

sneaked, snuck

The past form of **sneak** can be either **sneaked** or **snuck**. Some people object to **snuck**, but it is becoming more and more common in all North American writing and can be considered standard.

snuggly, snugly

Something cosy, soft, or comfortably warm is **snuggly**. Something that fits in a snug manner fits **snugly**: *It fits snugly in the box.*

so

The use of **so** to mean "very" or "extremely", as in *It's so cold today*, is considered informal. In formal writing, whenever you have an adjective after **so** (e.g. *so severe*), there should eventually be a **that** as well, as in *The following winter was so severe on the prairie that many starved before spring.*

soar, sore

To fly is to **soar**. Someone angry or in pain is **sore**.

soft-pedal

Note that the second part of **soft-pedal**, as in to *soft-pedal an issue*, is *pedal*, not *peddle* or *petal*.

solder

The metallic substance that is melted and used to join pipes or wires is **solder**, spelled with an *l* and only one *d*.

sole, soul

The spelling is **sole** for the undersurface of the foot, for the flatfish, and for "only". A person's spirit is their **soul**.

solely

⚠ Warning: There are two *l*'s in **solely**: *Bonuses are based solely on performance.*

soliloquy

⚠ Warning: the first part of **soliloquy** is spelled *sol-*, as in the word *solo*.

somersault

⚠ Warning: the word **somersault** does not include the word *summer*.

sore, soar

Someone angry or in pain is **sore**. To fly is to **soar**.

sow, sew

To plant seeds in a field is to **sow**; one can also *sow dissent*. To stitch is to **sew**.

speck, spec

A small dot or fleck is a **speck**. The spelling is **spec** for "specification" and in *on spec*.

split infinitives

Whether or not infinitives can be split by putting an adverb between the "to" and the verb is a very controversial question. The rule against splitting infinitives is not well founded, being based not on the actual workings of English but on Latin, a very different language. Still, the rule has been trumpeted as absolute for generations, to the point where even today split infinitives just sound "wrong" to many people. It is certainly true that in many cases split infinitives are less elegant, precise, or emphatic than alternative wordings, as in *We wanted to completely give up the business*, which is better rendered as *We wanted to give up the business completely*. But there are times when splitting an infinitive results in a clearer and more natural phrase than one with the adverb placed anywhere else, as in *You have to listen very closely to actually notice the difference*. Because of the controversy surrounding split infinitives, however, a prudent policy might be to split infinitives only when necessary for reasons of clarity, emphasis, or ease.

S

spur-of-the-moment, spur of the moment
Use hyphens when the phrase is used as an adjective, as in *It was a **spur-of-the-moment** decision*; otherwise do not: *We made the decision on the **spur of the moment***.

stake, steak
The spelling is **stake** for a sharpened stick, in wagering, in **stake out**, and in *what's at **stake?*** The cut of meat is a **steak**.

stair, stare
A flight of steps is a **staircase** or **stairs**; if you look intently, you **stare**.

stalk, stock
A stem is a **stalk**; to pursue is to **stalk**. The spelling is **stock** when you are speaking of supplies, merchandise, cattle, shares in a business, bouillon, rifles, or repertory theatre.

stationary, stationery
Something not moving is **stationary**. Writing materials are **stationery**. An easy way to remember this is that **stationery** has an *-er*, like *paper* and *letter*.

stayed, staid
The past tense of *stay* is **stayed**. A person or thing that is dull or unchanging is **staid**.

steak, stake
The cut of meat is a **steak**. The spelling is **stake** for a sharpened stick, in wagering, in **stake out**, and in *what's at **stake?***

steal, steel
To take something unjustly is to **steal**. The metal is **steel**.

sterling

⚠ Warning: **sterling** is spelled with an *e*, not an *i*: ***sterling*** *silver, pound* ***sterling***, *a* ***sterling*** *reputation*.

stock, stalk

The spelling is **stock** when you are speaking of supplies, merchandise, cattle, shares in a business, bouillon, rifles, or repertory theatre. A stem is a **stalk**; to pursue is to **stalk**.

straighten, straitened

Something made straight is **straightened**. If you are short of money you are living in **straitened** circumstances.

strait, straight

The spelling is **strait** for a narrow channel and in *dire* ***straits***; the usual spelling is **strait** in ***straitlaced*** and ***straitjacket***. Something not crooked is **straight**.

subject

G   a noun, noun phrase, or pronoun representing the person or thing that performs the action of the verb (*I* in *I sat down*), about which something is stated (*the house* in *The house is very old*), or, in a passive sentence, that is affected by the action of the verb (*the tree* in *The tree was blown down by the storm*).

subject-verb agreement

If the subject of your sentence is singular, the verb must also be singular; if the subject is plural, the verb must also be plural. The subject is not always the noun closest to the verb. Analyze your sentence carefully to identify the subject. In *Computers have revolutionized our lives*, 'computers' is the subject, and the verb is plural. But in *The advent of computers has revolutionized our lives* 'advent' is the subject and requires a singular verb. In *The Internet and mobile phone technology have had a profound impact*, the subject is two things, and requires a plural.

S

subjunctive

G (also **subjunctive mood**) a mood of verbs used to express a condition, wish, fear, possibility, command, suggestion or uncertainty, e.g. *if I were rich* or *I wish I were beautiful*.

G subordinate clause

a clause, usually introduced by a conjunction, that does not constitute a sentence itself but which depends on the principal clause that it modifies or in which it serves as a noun, e.g. *that she has come* in *I hope that she has come* or *because it was boring* in *She hated grammar because it was boring*. Subordinate clauses can come before, in the middle of, or after a main clause. Be careful not to use subordinate clauses alone without attaching them to a principal clause; this would be a SENTENCE FRAGMENT.

subordinating conjunction

G a conjunction that joins a subordinate clause to a main clause, e.g. *because* in *I am happy because it is sunny*. The most common subordinating conjunctions are: *after, although, as, as though, because, before, even though, ever since, however, if, if only, in case, lest, once, rather than, since, than, that, though, till, unless, until, whether, while*.

S

superlative

G (of an adjective or adverb) expressing the highest or a very high degree of a quality, e.g. *bravest, most fiercely*.

substitute

Avoid use of **substitute** with the prepositions *by* or *with*; use **for** instead. For example, reword **substitute** *sugar with honey* as **substitute** *honey* **for** *sugar*.

succeed, secede

When somebody becomes the rightful holder of a title or position, they **succeed** the person who formerly held the title or they **succeed** to the position itself: *Jamal* ***succeeded*** *Tracey as budget chief; Elizabeth* ***succeeded*** *to the throne in 1558.* A country or nation that officially leaves an alliance or federal union in order to become independent is said to **secede**: *In 1860, South Carolina became the first state to* ***secede*** *from the United States.*

succession, secession

The process in which a person takes over an official position or title is **succession**: *She's third in order of* ***succession*** *to the throne.* The withdrawal of a country or nation from an alliance or federal union in order to become independent is **secession**: *Demonstrators at a rally in Montreal urged Quebecers to vote against* ***secession***.

such

The use of **such** merely to emphasize a quality, as in *It was* ***such*** *a beautiful coat* or *We've had* ***such*** *awful weather*, is considered informal. In formal writing, this kind of construction should only be used if it is followed by a clause starting with *that*, as in *It was* ***such*** *a beautiful coat* ***that*** *Lois wanted one for herself* or *We've had* ***such*** *awful weather* ***that*** *I've hardly left the house.*

suffer

Although in modern English **suffer** is used almost exclusively to mean "experience something unpleasant", it is important to be aware of the word's archaic sense, "tolerate or allow", which is heard in certain set phrases that survive from the Bible or from older literature. For example, someone who does not ***suffer*** *fools gladly* is unwilling to put up with foolish people, and ***suffer*** *the little children* is part of a longer phrase, *suffer the little children to come unto me*, meaning "let the children come to me". It does not mean "the children ***suffer***", though it is much misused, especially as a journalistic cliché, in this way.

S

✗ **summersault** → **somersault** ✔
Warning: the word **somersault** (an acrobatic headfirst tumble) does not include the word *summer*.

summery, summary
Something reminiscent of summer is **summery**. A brief description of something is a **summary**.

Sunday, sundae
The day is **Sunday**. The dessert is a **sundae**.

supersede
Warning: **supersede** is spelled with an *s*, not with a *c*.

surf, serf
To ride the waves at a beach is to **surf**; **surf** is also the spelling in *surfing the Net*. A feudal labourer, e.g. in the Middle Ages, is a **serf**.

surprise
⚠ Warning: there are *two r's* in **surprise**.

sweet, suite
Something sugary is **sweet**. The spelling is **suite** for a set of furniture, a set of rooms in a hotel etc., and for a set of musical compositions.

sweetener
⚠ Warning: do not forget the *e* immediately before the *n* in **sweetener**.

symbol, cymbal
A design representing something is a **symbol**. The musical instrument is a **cymbal**.

synonym
G a word or expression that has the same or nearly the same meaning as another in the same language. Compare ANTONYM.

table

In Canada *to **table** a bill* usually means "to introduce a bill for discussion", especially in parliamentary contexts, while in the US it means "to set a bill aside indefinitely". Because of these contradictory senses, make sure your meaning is clear if you use the word, or use another word instead, e.g. **introduce** or **set aside**.

tariff

⚠ Warning: **tariff** is spelled with two *f*'s but only one *r*.

taught, taut

The past tense of *teach* is **taught**. The word for "tight" or "tense" is **taut**.

team, teem

A group of athletes etc. is a **team**. The spelling is **teem** in *teeming with fish* etc.

techy, tetchy

Something high-tech is **techy**. Someone who is irritable is **tetchy**.

teem, team

The spelling is **teem** in *teeming with fish* etc. A group of athletes etc. is a **team**.

tenant, tenet

⚠ Warning: do not double the first *n* of **tenant**. A **tenant** rents a place to live or work. A belief or principle held by a group or person is a **tenet**: *one of the basic **tenets** of Christianity*.

tense

G a form taken by a verb to indicate whether the action takes place in the past, present, or future, and whether it is completed or ongoing: *present tense*; *imperfect tense*.

tenterhook

⚠ Warning: **tenterhook** is spelled with a second *t*, not with a *d*. It does not include the word *tender*.

than

She's older than me (or *her* or *us*) is much more natural than *She's older than I* (or *she* or *we*), which can sound too formal. Because some people object to the common usage, however, consider adding a verb after **than**, e.g. *she's older than I am*, which nobody would criticize. Some circumstances require a distinction between *I* and *me* after **than**: *They like you better than I* means "they like you better **than** I (do)", whereas *They like you better **than** me* means "they like you better than (they like) me".

than, then

Don't use **then** when making comparisons: *You're taller **than** your brother.*

thank you, thank-you

Note that the spelling **thank-you**, with a hyphen, is used only in phrases like *a **thank-you** note, a **thank-you** letter, **thank-you** cards*. In all other situations, **thank you** is spelled without the hyphen: *I'm calling to **thank you** for looking after the cats while I was away; I'd like to say **thank you** for that money you lent me; I'm well, **thank you**, how are you?*

thankfully

Even in edited writing, **thankfully** is now by far more commonly used to mean "fortunately" or "thank goodness", as in ***Thankfully**, prices are dropping*, than to mean "with thanks", as in *They received the gifts **thankfully***. If you use the more widespread sense, you may find yourself criticized by those who still insist that the older usage is the only acceptable one, but this objection is being heard less and less often.

their, there, they're

The spelling is **their** for "belonging to them." The spelling is **there** in *I've been **there*** etc. The spelling **they're** is a contraction of *they are*: ***They're** putting **their** coats over **there***.

their

The use of the plural adjective **their** to mean "his or her" in sentences like *Everyone lost **their** temper* has become standard in spoken English and is becoming increasingly common in written English, especially when referring to words like *anyone* and *somebody*. Still, there are some people who object strongly to this use of **their**. To be safe you might consider arranging your sentences to avoid the issue altogether, e.g. *Everyone became short-tempered*.

theirs, there's

Note that there is no apostrophe in **theirs**: *It's not mine, it's **theirs***. **There's** means "there is", as in ***There's** certainly a lot of snow on the ground right now*.

them

Sentences like *If anyone shows up, ask **them** to wait*, and *Let everyone help **themselves***, have become standard in spoken English and are becoming increasingly common in written English. Still, there are some people who object strongly, saying that **them** and **themselves** are plural, whereas *anyone* and *everyone* are singular. To be safe you might consider arranging your sentences to avoid the issue altogether, e.g. *Let all your guests help **themselves*** or *If people show up, ask **them** to wait*.

them, they

The use of **them** instead of **they** after the verb *to be*, as in *It's **them** again*, is now considered acceptable in writing as well as speech. In sentences like *It is **they** who know you best*, however, **they** must be used instead of **them**. To avoid sounding excessively formal, such a sentence could be reworded *They're the ones who know you best*, which is much more natural. See also THAN.

themselves

Do not misuse **themselves**. Sentences like *Their employees and themselves have complained* and *We have received complaints from their employees and themselves* are not recommended. It is better to say *They and their employees have complained* and *We have received complaints from them and their employees*. Reserve **themselves** for reflexive uses like *They helped **themselves** to ice cream* or emphatic ones like *They **themselves** went through the same situation only months earlier*. It is not standard English to use the form "theirselves".

then, than

Don't use **then** when making comparisons: *You're taller **than** your brother*.

there, their, they're

The spelling is **there** in *I've been **there*** etc. The spelling is **their** for "belonging to them". The spelling **they're** is a contraction of *they are*: ***They're** putting **their** coats over **there***.

there

In careful writing, never use constructions like *There's four left*, where **there is** is followed by a plural; instead write ***There are** four left*. **There is** should only be followed by a singular: ***There's** one left*.

therefore

Be careful to use correct punctuation when you use **therefore**. The following are all correct:

When fighting a war, you know in advance that there will

be casualties to look after; **therefore,** *arrangements have to be made to accommodate the wounded.*

(make sure you use a semicolon, not a comma, before **therefore** and a comma after it)

The deficit has been a concern for Canadians for years. **Therefore***, the government has decided to spend some of the surplus in paying down the debt.*

(don't forget the comma after **therefore**)

Problems in such areas, **therefore***, may be alleviated by increased ventilation*

(since **therefore** is not introducing a new clause containing a subject and verb, it is just set off from the rest of the sentence by commas).

there's, theirs
There's means "there is", as in **There's** *certainly a lot of snow on the ground right now*. **Theirs** is a possessive pronoun meaning "the one that belongs to or is associated with them", as in *You can't take that stuff home with you—it's* **theirs**. There is no apostrophe in **theirs**.

they're, there, their
The spelling **they're** is a contraction of *they are*. The spelling is **there** in *I've been* **there** etc. The spelling is **their** for "belonging to them": **They're** *putting* **their** *coats over* **there**.

they
The use of the plural pronoun **they** to mean "he or she" in sentences like *Anyone can come along if* **they** *want to* has become standard in spoken English and is becoming increasingly common in written English, especially when referring to words like *anyone* and *somebody*. Still, there are some people who object strongly to this use of **they**. To be safe you might consider arranging your sentences to avoid the issue altogether, e.g. *Anyone who wants to can come along.*

thing

Instead of using the word **thing**, try to use more precise and interesting words:

> She is known for many remarkable **accomplishments**.
> That was the most puzzling **aspect** of the situation.
> What is the most distinctive **characteristic** of this bird?
> I want to know every **detail** of what happened.
> Smog is a **feature** of city life.
> She has campaigned on many controversial **issues**.
> We have several important **matters** to go over.
> The main **objective** is to save the money you make.
> She has a **penchant** for champagne and chocolate.
> You made an interesting **point**.
> Agility is an essential **quality** for a goalie.
> We discussed a number of **subjects**.
> The book covers a wide range of **topics**.
> Her generosity is one of her most attractive **traits**.

To avoid wordiness, don't use **thing** after an adjective when the adjective can be used on its own: *Having your own computer is very useful* (not *Having your own computer is a very useful thing*).

thought out, thought-out

Note the difference in spelling between *The strategy was clearly **thought out*** and *a clearly **thought-out** strategy*. There is a hyphen when the latter kind of structure is used.

threshold

⚠ Warning: there is only one *h* after the *s* in **threshold**.

throw, throe

To launch with the arm is to **throw**. The spelling is **throe** in *death **throes*** and *in the **throes** of*.

thusly

Thusly is generally regarded as an unnecessary synonym for **thus** and should be avoided.

till, until

Both **till** and **until** are perfectly acceptable, though only **until** is used at the beginning of a sentence: *I'll just relax* **until** (or **till**) *they arrive*. **Until** *they get here there's nothing I can do*.

timber, timbre

Wood and trees are **timber**. The quality of a sound is its **timbre**.

time, thyme

A clock measures **time**. The herb is **thyme**.

to, too, two

The spelling is **to** in *go* **to** *bed*, *come* **to** (i.e. regain consciousness), and before a verb (**to** *dream*). The spelling is **too** in **too** *much* and *I like it* **too**. The number is spelled **two**.

toe, tow

The spelling is **toe** in **toe** *the line*. To pull is to **tow**.

ton, tonne

Ton is used for various units of weight or volume, most commonly for a unit of 2,000 pounds. A **metric ton** is equivalent to 1,000 kg, and is also referred to as a **tonne**. The phrase *metric tonne* is redundant, since a **tonne** is always metric.

too, to, two

The spelling is **too** in **too** *much* and *I like it* **too**. The spelling is **to** in *go* **to** *bed*, *come* **to** (i.e. regain consciousness), and before a verb (**to** *dream*). The number is spelled **two**.

tool, tulle

An implement is a **tool**. A soft fine net for veils and tutus is **tulle**.

tortuous, torturous

Do not confuse **torturous**, which describes something considered a torture (*a **torturous** ordeal*), with **tortuous**, which describes something twisty, complex, or not straightforward (*a **tortuous** road*).

tot, taught, taut

A child or a dram of liquor is a **tot**. A tightened rope or a tense muscle is **taut**. The past tense of *teach* is **taught**.

tow, toe

To pull is to **tow**. The spelling is **toe** in *toe the line*.

toward, towards

Toward and **towards** are equally common in Canada—you can use them interchangeably.

tragedy

⚠ Warning: there is no *d* immediately before the *g* in **tragedy**.

transitive

G (of a verb or sense of a verb) that takes a direct object (whether expressed or implied).

tricep, triceps

Although **tricep** is becoming more common, it is still considered informal. **Triceps** remains the standard form for both the singular noun and its plural.

troop, troupe

A group of soldiers or scouts (or of people generally) is a **troop**. A company of actors or dancers is a **troupe**.

trooper, trouper

The spelling is **trooper** for a soldier, a police officer, and in *a real **trooper***. A performer in a theatre troupe is a **trouper**.

truly
⚠ Warning: there is no *e* in **truly**.

two, too, to
The number is **two**. The spelling is **too** in **too** *much* and *I like it* **too**. The spelling is **to** in *go* **to** *bed*, *come* **to** (i.e. regain consciousness), and before a verb (**to** *dream*).

Ukrainian
⚠ Warning: remember the *i* immediately before the first *n* in **Ukrainian**.

uncountable noun
G a noun that cannot form a plural or be used with the indefinite article, e.g. *happiness*.

underprivileged
⚠ Warning: there is no *d* before the *g* in **underprivileged**; do not forget the *i* before the *l*.

unexceptional, unexceptionable
Do not confuse **unexceptionable** and **unexceptional**: *Her new book is* **unexceptionable** means it contains nothing that would cause objections, while *Her new book is* **unexceptional** means it is mediocre.

unforeseen
⚠ Warning: do not forget the *e* immediately following the *r* in **unforeseen**.

unique
There has been much opposition to phrases such as **very unique** on the grounds that the original meaning of **unique**, "one of a kind", is absolute—something is either unique or it isn't, and nothing can be more or less unique than something else. While the newer informal sense of **unique** as "remarkable" or "unusual" can be qualified by adjectives like *very*, many people consider this use

incorrect, so you should avoid it in careful writing and speech.

unparalleled
⚠ Note that in **unparalleled** the first *l* is doubled but the *r* and the last *l* are not.

unwanted, unwonted
Something nobody wants is **unwanted**. Something that is not usual or expected is **unwonted**: *She spoke with **unwonted** enthusiasm.*

up-to-date, up to date
Note the difference in spelling between *up-to-date technology* and *The technology is **up to date***. There is no hyphen when the latter kind of structure is used.

us, we
The use of **us** instead of **we** after the verb *to be*, as in *It's **us** again*, is now considered acceptable in writing as well as speech. In sentences like *It is **we** who know you best*, however, **we** must be used instead of **us**. To avoid sounding excessively formal, such a sentence could be reworded ***We're** the ones who know you best*, which is much more natural. See also THAN.

used to, didn't use to
Note that the negative form of **used to**, as in *We **used to** go up to the lake every weekend* is **didn't use to**, not *didn't used to*: *We **didn't use to** go up during the winter.*

utilize, utilization, use
The words **utilize** and **utilization** are sometimes used instead of the verb and noun **use** with the mistaken impression that **use** is a less formal or less technical word. In fact, **use** is never considered informal and is perfectly acceptable in formal contexts. It is also shorter and less awkward than **utilize** and **utilization**, and for this

reason **use** is the better choice in both writing and speech.

vain, vein, vane
The spelling is **vain** for conceited, futile, and *in **vain***. The spelling is **vein** for a blood vessel or a streak in a rock. The spelling is **vane** in *weather **vane***.

valance, valence
A short curtain is a **valance**. The chemistry term is **valence**.

vale, veil
A literary term for a valley is **vale**, which is used in the phrase ***vale** of tears*. A piece of light material worn to cover the head or face is a **veil**.

venal, venial
Do not confuse **venal** and **venial**. A person who is willing to accept bribes in return for dishonest conduct is **venal**. A sin that is forgivable is **venial**.

verb
G   a word used to indicate an action, state, or occurrence, and forming the main part of the predicate of a sentence, e.g. *hear, become, happen.*

verbal
Because **verbal** can refer either to words generally (whether written or spoken), or to spoken words in particular, it may be better to use phrases like **oral statement** instead of **verbal statement** to avoid ambiguity or perceived redundancy. There are some expressions, however, in which the use of **verbal** to mean "oral" is well established and perfectly acceptable, e.g. ***verbal** agreement*. Words derived from **verbal** (like **verbally**) should be used with the same care.

V

verbal noun

G a noun formed as an inflection of a verb and partly sharing its constructions, e.g. *smoking* in *smoking is forbidden*.

vertebra, vertebrae

The singular form is **vertebra**; the plural form is **vertebrae**.

veteran

Warning: **veteran** is spelled with two *e*'s.

vial, vile

A small vessel for medicine is a **vial**. Something disgusting is **vile**.

vice, vise

The spelling is **vice** for a bad habit and in *vice* squad and *vice-president* etc. Canadians usually spell the clamp **vise**.

vigour, invigorate, reinvigorate

Note that while **vigour** is spelled with a *u*, **invigorate** and **reinvigorate** are not.

vile, vial

Something disgusting is **vile**. A small vessel for medicine is a **vial**.

viscose, viscous

Viscose is a type of yarn or textile. Something sticky or glutinous is **viscous**.

vise, vice

Canadians usually spell the clamp **vise**. The spelling is **vice** for a bad habit and in *vice* squad and *vice-president* etc.

voice

G the form of a verb that shows whether the subject of a sentence performs the action (ACTIVE VOICE: *The kids **ate*** *the pie*) or is affected by the action (PASSIVE VOICE: *The pie was eaten by the kids*).

volt, vault
The unit of electromotive force is a **volt**. An arch, chamber, or leap is a **vault**.

waist, waste
The middle part of the body is the **waist**. Garbage is **waste**; if you use more of something than you need, you **waste** it; someone or something that gets smaller *wastes away*.

waitress
Server is now usually preferred to the noun **waitress**.

waive, wave
If you choose not to exercise your rights, you **waive** them. The spelling is **wave** in *wave goodbye*, *wave aside objections*, and *wave off a goal*.

waiver, waver
A document that clears someone of responsibility is a **waiver**; athletes are put on **waivers**. To be unsteady or undecided is to **waver**.

wanton, won ton
The spelling is **wanton** in *wanton destruction*. Someone who behaves in an immoral way is **wanton**. A Chinese dumpling is a **won ton**: *won ton soup*.

ware, wear
Articles for sale are **wares**; china, cutlery, etc. are *tableware*. The spelling is **wear** in *wear a hat* and *wear away the paint*; shoes etc. are *footwear*.

waste, waist
Garbage is **waste**; if you use more of something than you

need, you **waste** it; someone or something that gets smaller **wastes** *away*. The middle part of the body is the **waist**.

wave, waive
The spelling is **wave** in **wave** *goodbye*, **wave** *aside objections*, and **wave** *off a goal*. If you choose not to exercise your rights, you **waive** them.

waver, waiver
To be unsteady or undecided is to **waver**. A document that clears someone of responsibility is a **waiver**; athletes are put on **waivers**.

way, weigh, whey
A path or method is a **way**. To determine the heaviness of something is to **weigh** it. When milk forms curds the watery liquid that remains is **whey**.

weak, week
To be feeble is to be **weak**. Seven days is a **week**.

wear, ware
The spelling is **wear** in **wear** *a hat* and **wear** *away the paint*; shoes etc. are **footwear**. Articles for sale are **wares**; china, cutlery etc. are **tableware**.

week, weak
Seven days is a **week**. To be feeble is to be **weak**.

weird
⚠ Warning: **weird** is an exception to the "*i* before *e* except after *c*" rule. In **weird** the *e* comes before the *i*.

W

well
Combinations beginning with **well**, such as **well aimed**, are written as two separate words when following a verb, as in *That shot was **well aimed**,* but

with a hyphen when they come before a noun, as in *That was a **well-aimed** shot*.

went, gone
Never say *I should have went*. The correct form is *I should have **gone***.

wet, whet
Something soaked is **wet**. If you make someone hungry or eager for something, you **whet** their appetite.

whence, from whence
The expression **from whence** is considered redundant by many people on the grounds that **whence** already implies **from**. It's safer to say *They returned **whence** they came* than to say *They returned **from whence** they came*.

where, wear, ware
The spelling is **where** for "at which location" The spelling is **wear** in **wear** *a hat* and **wear** *away the paint*. Articles for sale are **wares**.

whereabouts
While **whereabouts** most commonly takes a plural verb, as in *Her **whereabouts** are not known*, it may also be used correctly with a singular verb: *The **whereabouts** of the purse and its contents remains a mystery*.

wherefore
The word **wherefore** means "why", not "where". Juliet's question, "**Wherefore** art thou Romeo?" does not mean, "Where are you, Romeo?" but "Why are you Romeo?", i.e. "Why are you who you are, the son of a family my family hates?"

W

which
If the clause introduced by **which** provides additional information about the noun it refers to but is not

essential in identifying it, a comma is necessary before **which** and at the end of the clause: *The picture,* **which** *was hanging above the fireplace, was a present.* If the information in the clause is necessary in identifying the preceding noun, no comma is required and **which** may be replaced by **that**: *The picture* **which/that** *was hanging above the fireplace was a present.*

which, witch
The spelling is **which** in *Which one?* and *your letter,* **which** *I read twice.* A sorceress or adherent of the Wiccan religion is a **witch**.

while, wile
The spelling is **while** in *while away the time,* as well as in *a short* **while** and **while** *that may be true.* A trick or lure is a **wile**.

whisky, whiskey
Whisky is the standard spelling used in Canada unless the drink being referred to is **Irish whiskey**; in the US the word is generally spelled **whiskey** except in **Scotch whisky**.

whit, to wit
A small amount is a **whit**: *They didn't pay a* **whit** *of attention.* There is no *h* in **to wit**, meaning "namely", as in *the attitudes of grunge,* **to wit***: angst, apathy, and boredom.*

who, whom
While it may be acceptable in informal speech to use **who** for the object of a verb or preposition, as in *Who did you see?*, *The teacher* **who** *I saw,* and *Who are you waiting for?*, you should always use the more standard **whom** in essays, formal speeches, etc. (*Whom did you see?*; *The teacher* **whom** *I saw; Whom are you waiting for?*), especially as the object of a preposition (*For* **whom** *will you vote?*). Sometimes, however,

W

a pronoun following a preposition is not the object of the preposition: in a sentence like *There was no announcement as to **who** will replace him,* the word **who** is the subject of the verb *will replace,* not the object of the preposition *to,* and so would be incorrect as **whom**.

wholly
Something that is owned completely or entirely is **wholly** owned.

whose, who's
Don't confuse **who's** and **whose**. If you mean "who is" or "who has" use **who's**, as in ***Who's** on first?* or ***Who's** been in the kitchen?* Use **whose** when using *who is* or *who has* instead would sound wrong, as in questions like ***Whose** is this?* or ***Whose** book is this?* and statements like *the child **whose** face was smeared with chocolate.*

wierd → weird ✔
Warning: **weird** is an exception to the "*i* before *e* except after *c*" rule. In **weird** the *e* comes before the *i*.

wile, while
A trick or lure is a **wile**. The spelling is **while** in ***while** away the time,* as well as in *a short **while*** and ***while** that may be true.*

windfall
Warning: do not forget the *d* in **windfall**.

wine, whine
Fermented grape juice is **wine**. When someone complains in an annoying voice they **whine**.

W

winey, whiny
Something having the taste or look of wine is **winey**. Someone who complains annoyingly is **whiny**.

-wise

Combinations using **-wise**, such as **salary-wise** in *I lowered my expectations **salary-wise,*** are quite often inelegant. Use them sparingly, if at all.

wit, whit

There is no *h* in **to wit**, meaning "namely", as in *the attitudes of grunge,* **to wit**: *angst, apathy, and boredom.* A small amount is a **whit**: *They didn't pay a **whit** of attention.*

witch, which

A sorceress or adherent of the Wiccan religion is a **witch**. The spelling is **which** in ***Which** one?* and *your letter, **which** I read twice.*

withdrawal

Warning: There are two *a*'s in **withdrawal**.

withhold

Be sure to double the *h* in **withhold**.

witness box, witness stand

The official Canadian term is **witness box**.

won ton, wanton

A Chinese dumpling is a **won ton**: ***won ton** soup.* Something that causes harm at random and without motive is **wanton**: ***wanton** destruction;* someone who behaves in an immoral way is **wanton**.

would

Do not say *If I **would** have been there I **would** have spoken my mind.* Use **would** only once, with the verb that is not introduced by *if*: *If I **had** been there I **would** have spoken my mind.*

would have

Note that in statements such as *You **would have** loved it,* the correct expression is **would have** (or the contraction **would've**) and not *would of*.

wrack, rack
Wrack is a type of seaweed or a wreck. Canadians prefer **rack** over **wrack** in *rack up points*, *rack your brains*, *rack and ruin*, and *nerve-racking*. The spelling is always **rack** in *storage rack* and *rack of lamb*.

wrapped, rapt
To be enveloped is to be **wrapped**. To be fully absorbed in something or carried away with feeling or thought is to be **rapt**.

wretch, retch
An unfortunate or wicked person is a **wretch**. To gag is to **retch**.

wringer, ringer
The spelling is **wringer** in *put through the wringer*. Two people who look very much alike are **dead ringers**.

write, rite
To put words on paper is to **write**. A religious observance is a **rite**.

yew, ewe
A **yew** is a tree. A female sheep is a **ewe**.

yoke, yolk
A harness or a burden is a **yoke**. The centre of an egg is a **yolk**.

W

you, ewe, yew
You is the second person pronoun. A female sheep is a **ewe**. The tree is a **yew**.

yourself

Do not misuse **yourself** or **yourselves**. Sentences like *The team and yourself will have a tough game tonight* and *There will be an assembly for your teachers and yourselves* are not recommended. It is better to say *You and the team will have a tough game tonight* and *There will be an assembly for you and your teachers*. Reserve **yourself** for reflexive uses like *You can help **yourself** to a drink* or emphatic ones like *You **yourself** had problems when you were her age*.

youse

Youse is a non-standard word and should be avoided in careful speech and writing. The form for both the singular and the plural is **you**.

Z

Both "zed" and "zee" are acceptable pronunciations for the letter **Z** in Canada, though "zed" is much more common. Be warned, however, that some people feel very strongly that it is a betrayal of Canadian nationality to say "zee" and you may incur their wrath if you do so.

Z

Appendix 1: Punctuation and Capitalization

Punctuation is used to separate strings of words into manageable groups and help clarify their meaning. The marks most commonly used to divide a piece of prose or other writing are the period, the semicolon, and the comma, with the strength of the dividing or separating role diminishing from the period to the comma. The period marks the main division into sentences; the semicolon joins sentences (as in this sentence); and the comma (which is the most flexible in use and causes the most problems) separates smaller elements with the least loss of continuity. Brackets and dashes also serve as separators–often more strikingly than commas, as in this sentence.

period .

- A period is used to mark the end of a sentence that is not a question or exclamation. In prose, sentences marked by periods normally represent an independent or distinct statement; more closely connected or complementary statements are joined by a semicolon (as here).

- Periods are used to mark abbreviations (*Wed., Gen., p.m.*). They are often omitted in abbreviations that consist entirely of capital letters (*CBC, EDT, RRSP*), and in acronyms that are pronounced as a word rather than a sequence of letters (*Intelsat*), and should be omitted in abbreviations for SI units (*Hz, kg, cm*).

- If an abbreviation with a period comes at the end of a sentence, another period is not added:

  They have a collection of many animals, including dogs, cats, tortoises, snakes, etc.

but

They have a collection of many animals (dogs, cats, tortoises, snakes, etc.).

- A period is used as a decimal point (*10.5%, $1.65*), and to separate the domains of an email or Web address (*www.oup.com*). It is commonly used in British practice to divide hours and minutes in giving time (*6.15 p.m.*), where a colon is standard in North American use.

semicolon   ;

- The main role of the semicolon is to join sentences that are closely related or that parallel each other in some way, as in the following:

Many new houses are being built north of the city; areas to the south are still largely industrial.

To err is human; to forgive, divine.

- It is often used as a stronger division in a sentence that already includes several commas:

Joanne and Emily went out for dinner, as they usually did on Wednesday; but when, upon arriving at the restaurant, they were told they would have to wait for a table, they went home and ordered Chinese.

- It is used in a similar way in lists of names or other items to indicate a stronger division:

I would like to thank the managing director, Jennifer Dunbar; my secretary, Raymond Martin; and my assistant, David Singh.

comma   ,

- Use of the comma is more difficult to describe than other punctuation marks, and there is considerable variation in practice. Essentially, it is used to give structure to sentences, especially longer ones, and make their meaning clear. Too many commas can be distracting; too few can make a piece of writing difficult to read or, worse, difficult to understand.

- A comma is used to separate the main clauses of a sentence, often followed by a conjunction such as *and, but,* or *yet:*

  Mario cooked a roast, and Jan baked a pie for dessert.

  A comma is not used when the subject of the first clause is understood to be the subject of the second clause:

  Mario cooked a roast and baked a pie for dessert.

- It is considered incorrect to join the clauses of a compound sentence without a conjunction. The following sentence:

  I like skating very much, I go to the local rink every day after school.

  should be rewritten as

  I like skating very much; I go to the local rink every day after school.

  or as

  I like skating very much, and I go to the local rink every day after school.

- It is also considered incorrect to separate a subject from its verb with a comma:

  Those with the smallest incomes and no other means, should get more support.

  should be rewritten as

  Those with the smallest incomes and no other means should get more support.

- Commas are usually inserted between adjectives coming before a noun:

  An enterprising, ambitious person.

  A cold, damp, poorly heated room.

  But the comma is omitted when the last adjective has a closer relation to the noun than the others:

  A distinguished foreign politician.

  A noisy blue jay.

- An important role of the comma is to prevent ambiguity. Imagine how the following sentences might be interpreted without the comma:

  With the police pursuing, the people shouted loudly.

  She did not want to leave, from a feeling of loyalty.

  In the valley below, the houses appeared very small.

- Commas are used in pairs to separate elements in a sentence that are not part of the main statement:

  I would like you all, ladies and gentlemen, to raise your glasses.

  There is no truth, as far as I can see, to this rumour.

  It appears, however, that we were wrong.

- A comma is also used to separate a relative clause from a noun when the clause is used to provide additional information about the noun but is not essential in identifying it (a non-defining or non-restrictive relative clause):

  The picture, which was hanging above the fireplace, was a present.

  In the above sentence, the information in the *which* clause is incidental to the main statement. Without the commas, it would form an essential part of the statement in identifying which picture is being referred to (and *which* could be replaced by *that*); this is a defining or restrictive relative clause:

The picture which/that was hanging above the fireplace was a present.

- Commas are used to separate items in a list or sequence:

  Emma, Sheilah, and Dorcas went out for lunch.

  The doctor told me to go home, get some rest, and drink plenty of fluids.

  It is acceptable to omit the final comma before *and*; however, the final comma has the advantage of clarifying the grouping at a composite name occurring at the end of a list:
  I buy my art supplies at Midoco, Loomis and Toles, and Grand and Toy.

- A comma is often used in numbers of four or more digits to separate each group of three consecutive digits starting from the right (e.g. *10,135,793*). In metric practice, a space is used instead of a comma to separate each group of three consecutive figures (*10 135 793*).

- A comma is used to introduce a quotation of a complete sentence:

  Joan exclaimed, "Isn't he fabulous!"

  and substitutes for a period at the end of a quotation if this is followed by a continuation of the sentence:

  "I've never seen such a fabulous dancer," said Joan.

colon   :

- The main role of the colon is to separate main clauses when there is a step forward from the first to the second, especially from introduction to main point, from general statement to example, from cause to effect, and from premise to conclusion:

There is something I forgot to tell you: your mother called earlier.

It was not easy: to begin with, we had to raise the necessary capital.

- It also introduces a list of items (do not use a dash for this purpose):

This recipe requires the following: semi-sweet chocolate, cream, egg whites, and sugar.

- It is used to introduce, more formally and emphatically than a comma would, speech or quoted material:

I told them last week: "Do not under any circumstances open this box."

- It is used to divide hours and minutes in giving time (*6:30 p.m., 18:30*).

question mark ?

- A question mark is used in place of a period to show that the preceding sentence is a question:

She actually volunteered to do it?

Would you like another cup of coffee?

It is not used when the question is implied by indirect speech:

I asked you if you would like another cup of coffee.

- It is used (often in brackets) to express doubt or uncertainty about a word or phrase immediately following or preceding it:

Jean Talon, born (?) 1625.

They were then seen boarding a bus (to Kingston?).

exclamation mark   !

- An exclamation mark is used after an exclamatory word, phrase, or sentence expressing any of the following:

- Absurdity:
  That's preposterous!

- Command or warning:
  Watch out!

- Contempt or disgust:
  Your hands are filthy!

- Emotion or pain:
  I love this song!
  Ouch! That hurts!

- Enthusiasm:
  I can't wait to see you!

- Wish or regret:
  If only I could fly!

- Wonder, admiration, or surprise:
  Isn't that beautiful!

apostrophe   '

- The main use of an apostrophe is to indicate the possessive case, as in *Julie's book* or *the boys' mother.* It comes before the *s* in singular and plural nouns not ending in *s,* as in *the girl's costumes* and *the women's costumes.* It comes after the *s* in plural nouns ending in *s,* as in *the girls' costumes.*

- In singular nouns ending in *s* practice differs between (for example) *Charles'* and *Charles's*; in some cases the shorter form is preferable for reasons of sound, as in *Xerxes' fleet* or *in Jesus' name*.

- It is also used to indicate a place or business, e.g. *the baker's*.

- It is used to indicate that a letter or series of letters has been removed to form a contraction, e.g. *we're, mustn't, Hallowe'en, o'clock*.

- It is sometimes used to form a plural of individual letters or numbers, although this use is diminishing. It is helpful in *dot your i's and cross your t's,* but unnecessary in *MPs* and *1940s*.

---

quotation marks   " "

- The main use of quotation marks is to indicate direct speech and quotations. Quotation marks are used at the beginning and end of quoted material:

  She said, "I have something to tell you."

  The closing quotation marks should come after any punctuation mark which is part of the quoted matter, but before any mark which is not:

  They shouted, "Watch out!", but it was too late.

  They were described as "an unruly bunch".

  Punctuation dividing a sentence of quoted speech is put inside the quotation marks:

- *"Go away," he said, "and don't ever come back."*

  Quotation marks are also placed around cited words and phrases:

  What does "integrated circuit" mean?

- A quotation within a quotation is put in single quotation marks:

"Have you any idea," he asked, "what 'integrated circuit' means?"

This is the practice followed by most North American publishers. British publishers use single quotation marks for a first quotation and double quotation marks for a quotation within:

'Have you any idea,' he asked, 'what "integrated circuit" means?'

brackets (parentheses)

- The types of brackets used in normal punctuation are round brackets ( ), also known as parentheses, and square brackets [ ]. The main use of round brackets is to enclose explanations and extra information or comment:

He was (and still is) a rebel.

Congo (formerly Zaire).

He spoke at length about his Weltanschauung *(world view).*

- They are used to give references and citations:

Wilfrid Laurier (1841–1919).

A discussion of integrated circuits (see p. 38).

- They are used to enclose optional words:

There are many (apparent) difficulties.

(In this example, the difficulties may or may not be only apparent.)

- Square brackets are used less often. The main use is to enclose extra information added by someone (normally an editor) other than the writer of the surrounding text:

Robert walked in, and his sister [Sara] greeted him.

- They are sometimes used to enclose extra information within text that is already in round brackets:

Robert and Rebecca entered the room, and Sara greeted them. (Robert and Rebecca had concluded a three-week driving adventure [through Quebec] and had not seen Sara in some time.)

dash

- A single dash is used to indicate a pause, either to represent a hesitation in speech or to introduce an explanation of what comes before it:

We must try to help—before it's too late.

- A pair of dashes is used to enclose an aside or additional piece of information, like the use of commas as explained above, but forming a more distinct break:

He refused to tell anyone—least of all his wife—about that embarrassing moment during the medical exam.

- It is sometimes used to indicate an omitted word or a portion of an omitted word, for example a coarse or offensive word in reported speech:

"They were p—off," he said.

- It is also used to sum up a list before carrying on with a sentence:

Chocolates, flowers, champagne—any of these would be appreciated.

Because many keyboards do not have a dash, two hyphens, with no space before or after, can be used to make a dash.

hyphen

-

- The hyphen has two main functions: to link words to form longer words and compounds, and to mark the division of a word at the end of a line in print or writing.

- The use of the hyphen to connect words to form compound words is diminishing in English. It is often retained to avoid awkward collisions of letters (as in *twist-tie, re-emerge,* or *mis-hit*) or to distinguish a word like *re-sign* from *resign.*

- The hyphen serves to connect words that have a syntactic link, as in *soft-centred candies* and *French-speaking people,* where the reference is to candies with soft centres and people who speak French, rather than soft candies with centres and French people who can speak (which would be the sense conveyed if the hyphens were omitted). It is also used to avoid more extreme kinds of ambiguity, as in *twenty-odd people.*

- A particularly important use of the hyphen is to link compounds and phrases used attributively, as in *a well-known man* (but *the man is well known*), *water-cooler gossip* (but *gossip around the water cooler*), and a *sold-out show* (but *the show is sold out*).

- A hyphen is often used to turn a phrasal verb into a noun:

  She injured her shoulder in the warm-up before the game.

  Notice however that while a hyphen is used in the noun, the verb is still spelled without a hyphen:

  Stretching is a good way to warm up before a game.

- It is used to indicate a common second element in all but the last of a list, e.g. *two-, three-,* or *fourfold.*

- The hyphen used to divide a word at the end of a line is a different matter, because it is not a permanent feature of the spelling. The general principle to follow is to insert the hyphen where it will least distract the reader, usually at a syllable break.

...

ellipsis

- A sequence of three periods is used to mark an ellipsis or omission in a sequence of words, especially when forming an incomplete quotation. When the omission occurs at the end of a sentence, a fourth point is added as the period of the whole sentence:

  He left the room, slammed the door...and went out.

  The report said: "There are many issues to be considered, of which the most important are money, time, and personnel....Let us consider personnel first."

A

capital letter

- A capital letter is used for the first letter of the word beginning a sentence:

  She decided not to come. Later she changed her mind.

- A sentence contained in brackets within a larger sentence does not normally begin with a capital letter:

  I have written several letters (there are many to be written) and hope to finish them tomorrow.

  In the following, however, the sentence is a separate one and therefore it does begin with a capital letter:

  We have more than one option. (You have said this often before.) So we should think carefully before acting.

- A capital letter also begins sentences that form quoted

speech:

The assistant turned and replied, "We think it works."

- The use of capital letters to distinguish proper nouns or names from ordinary words is subject to wide variation in practice. Some guidelines are offered here, but the most important criterion is consistency within a single piece of writing.

  Capital letters are used for:

  > the names of people and places (*Terry Fox, Prince Edward Island, Robson Street*)

  > the names of languages, peoples, and words derived from these (*Inuktitut, Vietnamese, Quebecer, Englishwoman, Americanism*)

  > the names of institutions and organizations (*the Crown, the Senate, the Department of Health, the National Museum of Natural Sciences, the Law Society of Upper Canada*)

  > the names of religions and their adherents (*Judaism, Muslim, the United Church*)

  > the names of months and days (*June, Monday, New Year's Day*)

  > nouns or abstract qualities personified (*a victim of Fate*)

- Note that *the Anglican Church* is an institution, but *the Anglican church* is a building; a *Democrat* belongs to a political party, but a *democrat* simply supports democracy; *Northern Ireland* is a name with recognized status, but *northern England* is not.

- A capital letter is used by convention in many names that are trademarks (*Xerox, Cineplex, Arborite*) or are otherwise associated with a particular manufacturer.

Verbs derived from such proprietary terms are often not capitalized (*xeroxing, googled, skidooing*).

- Capital letters are used in titles of courtesy or rank, including compound titles, when these directly precede a name (*the Right Honourable Lester B. Pearson, Dame Emma Albani, Brigadier General Daigle, Prime Minister Paul Martin*).

- It is not necessary to capitalize a title when it is not placed directly before a name or when it is set off by commas (*an interview with Paul Martin, prime minister of Canada; an interview with the prime minister, Paul Martin*).

- A capital letter is used for the name of a deity (*God, Father, Allah, Great Spirit*). However, the use of capitals in possessive adjectives and possessive pronouns (*in His name*) is now generally considered old-fashioned.

- Capital letters are used for the first and other important words in titles of books, newspapers, plays, movies, and television programs (*The Merchant of Venice, Who Has Seen the Wind, Guide to the Use of the Dictionary, Hockey Night in Canada*).

- Capital letters are used for historical events and periods (*the Dark Ages, the Renaissance, the First World War*); also for geological time divisions, but not for certain archaeological periods (*Devonian, Paleozoic,* but *neolithic*).

- Capital letters are frequently used in abbreviations, with or without periods (*CTV, M.B.A.*).

- A capital letter is used for a compass direction when abbreviated (*N, NE, NNE*) or when denoting a region (*cold weather in the North*).

Appendix 2: Irregular Verbs

Infinitive	3rd Person Singular Present	Past Tense	Past Participle	Present Participle
abide	abides	abided	abided	abiding
arise	arises	arose	arisen	arising
awake	awakes	awoke	awoken	awaking
babysit	babysits	babysat	babysat	babysitting
backlight	backlights	backlit, backlighted	backlit, backlighted	backlighting
backslide	backslides	backslid	backslid	backsliding
be	is	was/were	been	being
bear	bears	bore	borne	bearing
beat	beats	beat	beaten	beating
become	becomes	became	become	becoming
befall	befalls	befell	befallen	befalling
beget	begets	begat, begot	begotten	begetting
begin	begins	began	begun	beginning
behold	beholds	beheld	beheld	beholding
bend	bends	bent	bent	bending
beseech	beseeches	beseeched, besought	beseeched, besought	beseeching
beset	besets	beset	beset	besetting
bespeak	bespeaks	bespoke	bespoken	bespeaking

Infinitive	3rd Person Singular Present	Past Tense	Past Participle	Present Participle
bestride	bestrides	bestrode	bestridden	bestriding
bet	bets	bet, betted	bet, betted	betting
bid	bids	bid, bade	bid, bidden	bidding
bind	binds	bound	bound	binding
bite	bites	bit	bitten	biting
bivouac	bivouacs	bivouacked	bivouacked	bivouacking
bleed	bleeds	bled	bled	bleeding
blow	blows	blew	blown	blowing
break	breaks	broke	broken	breaking
breed	breeds	bred	bred	breeding
bring	brings	brought	brought	bringing
broadcast	broadcasts	broadcast	broadcast	broadcasting
browbeat	browbeats	browbeat	browbeaten	browbeating
build	builds	built	built	building
burn	burns	burned, burnt	burned, burnt	burning
burst	bursts	burst	burst	bursting
bust	busts	busted, bust	busted, bust	busting
buy	buys	bought	bought	buying
cast	casts	cast	cast	casting
catch	catches	caught	caught	catching

Infinitive	3rd Person Singular Present	Past Tense	Past Participle	Present Participle
cha-cha	cha-chas	cha-chaed	cha-chaed	cha-chaing
choose	chooses	chose	chosen	choosing
cleave (split)	cleaves	cleaved, clove, cleft	cloven, cleft, cleaved	cleaving
cleave (adhere)	cleaves	cleaved	cleaved	cleaving
cling	clings	clung	clung	clinging
come	comes	came	come	coming
cost (have as a price)	costs	cost	cost	costing
cost (estimate price)	costs	costed	costed	costing
creep	creeps	crept	crept	creeping
crossbreed	crossbreeds	crossbred	crossbred	crossbreeding
crosscut	crosscuts	crosscut	crosscut	crosscutting
crow	crows	crowed, crew	crowed, crew	crowing
cut	cuts	cut	cut	cutting
deal	deals	dealt	dealt	dealing
DH	DH's	DH'd	DH'd	DH'ing
dig	digs	dug	dug	digging
dive	dives	dived, dove	dived	diving
do	does	did	done	doing
draw	draws	drew	drawn	drawing
dream	dreams	dreamt, dreamed	dreamt, dreamed	dreaming

Infinitive	3rd Person Singular Present	Past Tense	Past Participle	Present Participle
drink	drinks	drank	drunk	drinking
drive	drives	drove	driven	driving
dwell	dwells	dwelt, dwelled	dwelt, dwelled	dwelling
eat	eats	ate	eaten	eating
fall	falls	fell	fallen	falling
feed	feeds	fed	fed	feeding
feel	feels	felt	felt	feeling
fight	fights	fought	fought	fighting
find	finds	found	found	finding
fit	fits	fitted, fit	fitted, fit	fitting
flee	flees	fled	fled	fleeing
fling	flings	flung	flung	flinging
floodlight	floodlights	floodlit	floodlit	floodlighting
fly	flies	flew, flied	flew, flied	flying
forbear	forbears	forbore	forborne	forbearing
forbid	forbids	forbade	forbidden	forbidding
forecast	forecasts	forecast	forecast	forecasting
foreknow	foreknows	foreknew	foreknown	foreknowing
foresee	foresees	foresaw	foreseen	foreseeing
foretell	foretells	foretold	foretold	foretelling

Infinitive	3rd Person Singular Present	Past Tense	Past Participle	Present Participle
forget	forgets	forgot	forgotten	forgetting
forgive	forgives	forgave	forgiven	forgiving
forgo	forgoes	forwent	forgone	forgoing
forsake	forsakes	forsook	forsaken	forsaking
freeze	freezes	froze	frozen	freezing
frolic	frolics	frolicked	frolicked	frolicking
FTP	FTP's	FTP'd	FTP'd	FTP'ing
gainsay	gainsays	gainsaid	gainsaid	gainsaying
get	gets	got	got, gotten	getting
give	gives	gave	given	giving
go	goes	went	gone	going
grind	grinds	ground	ground	grinding
grow	grows	grew	grown	growing
hamstring	hamstrings	hamstrung	hamstrung	hamstringing
hang (suspend)	hangs	hung	hung	hanging
hang (be executed)	hangs	hanged	hanged	hanging
have	has	had	had	having
hear	hears	heard	heard	hearing
heave	heaves	heaved, hove	heaved, hove	heaving
hew	hews	hewed	hewn, hewed	hewing

Infinitive	3rd Person Singular Present	Past Tense	Past Participle	Present Participle
hide (*conceal*)	hides	hid	hidden	hiding
hit	hits	hit	hit	hitting
hold	holds	held	held	holding
hurt	hurts	hurt	hurt	hurting
inbreed	inbreeds	inbred	inbred	inbreeding
inlay	inlays	inlaid	inlaid	inlaying
input	inputs	input, inputted	input, inputted	inputting
inset	insets	inset	inset	insetting
intercut	intercuts	intercut	intercut	intercutting
interweave	interweaves	interwove	interwoven	interweaving
keep	keeps	kept	kept	keeping
kneel	kneels	knelt, kneeled	knelt, kneeled	kneeling
knit	knits	knitted, knit	knitted, knit	knitting
know	knows	knew	known	knowing
KO	KO's	KO'd	KO'd	KO'ing
lade	lades	laded	laden	lading
lay	lays	laid	laid	laying
lead	leads	led	led	leading
lean	leans	leaned, leant	leaned, leant	leaning
leap	leaps	leaped, leapt	leaped, leapt	leaping

Infinitive	3rd Person Singular Present	Past Tense	Past Participle	Present Participle
learn	learns	learned, learnt	learned, learnt	learning
leave	leaves	left	left	leaving
lend	lends	lent	lent	lending
let	lets	let	let	letting
lie (rest)	lies	lay	lain	lying
light (set alight)	lights	lit	lit, lighted	lighting
light (come upon)	lights	lit, lighted	lit, lighted	lighting
lose	loses	lost	lost	losing
make	makes	made	made	making
MC	MC's	MC'd	MC'd	MC'ing
mean	means	meant	meant	meaning
medevac	medevacs	medevacked	medevacked	medevacking
meet	meets	met	met	meeting
mimic	mimics	mimicked	mimicked	mimicking
miscast	miscasts	miscast	miscast	miscasting
misdeal	misdeals	misdealt	misdealt	misdealing
mishear	mishears	misheard	misheard	mishearing
mislay	mislays	mislaid	mislaid	mislaying
mislead	misleads	misled	misled	misleading
misread	misreads	misread	misread	misreading

Infinitive	3rd Person Singular Present	Past Tense	Past Participle	Present Participle
misspell	misspells	misspelled, misspelt	misspelled, misspelt	misspelling
misspend	misspends	misspent	misspent	misspending
mistake	mistakes	mistook	mistaken	mistaking
misunderstand	misunderstands	misunderstood	misunderstood	misunderstanding
mow	mows	mowed	mowed, mown	mowing
narrowcast	narrowcasts	narrowcast	narrowcast	narrowcasting
OD	OD's	OD'd	OD'd	OD'ing
offset	offsets	offset	offset	offsetting
OK	OK's	OK'd	OK'd	OK'ing
outbid	outbids	outbid	outbid	outbidding
outdo	outdoes	outdid	outdone	outdoing
outgrow	outgrows	outgrew	outgrown	outgrowing
output	outputs	output	output	outputting
outrun	outruns	outran	outrun	outrunning
outsell	outsells	outsold	outsold	outselling
outshine	outshines	outshone	outshone	outshining
outshoot	outshoots	outshot	outshot	outshooting
outspend	outspends	outspent	outspent	outspending
outspread	outspreads	outspread	outspread	outspreading
overcome	overcomes	overcame	overcome	overcoming

Infinitive	3rd Person Singular Present	Past Tense	Past Participle	Present Participle
overcut	overcuts	overcut	overcut	overcutting
overdo	overdoes	overdid	overdone	overdoing
overdraw	overdraws	overdrew	overdrawn	overdrawing
overeat	overeats	overate	overeaten	overeating
overfeed	overfeeds	overfed	overfed	overfeeding
overfly	overflies	overflew	overflown	overflying
overhang	overhangs	overhung	overhung	overhanging
overhear	overhears	overheard	overheard	overhearing
overlay	overlays	overlaid	overlaid	overlaying
overlie	overlies	overlay	overlain	overlying
overpay	overpays	overpaid	overpaid	overpaying
override	overrides	overrode	overridden	overriding
overrun	overruns	overran	overrun	overrunning
oversee	oversees	oversaw	overseen	overseeing
oversell	oversells	oversold	oversold	overselling
overshoot	overshoots	overshot	overshot	overshooting
oversleep	oversleeps	overslept	overslept	oversleeping
overspend	overspends	overspent	overspent	overspending
overtake	overtakes	overtook	overtaken	overtaking
overthrow	overthrows	overthrew	overthrown	overthrowing

Infinitive	3rd Person Singular Present	Past Tense	Past Participle	Present Participle
overwind	overwinds	overwound	overwound	overwinding
overwrite	overwrites	overwrote	overwritten	overwriting
panic	panics	panicked	panicked	panicking
partake	partakes	partook	partaken	partaking
pay	pays	paid	paid	paying
picnic	picnics	picnicked	picnicked	picnicking
plead	pleads	pleaded	pleaded	pleading
politic	politics	politicked	politicked	politicking
prepay	prepays	prepaid	prepaid	prepaying
proofread	proofreads	proofread	proofread	proofreading
prove	proves	proved	proven, proved	proving
put	puts	put	put	putting
quit	quits	quit	quit	quitting
read	reads	read	read	reading
rebroadcast	rebroadcasts	rebroadcast	rebroadcast	rebroadcasting
rebuild	rebuilds	rebuilt	rebuilt	rebuilding
recast	recasts	recast	recast	recasting
recut	recuts	recut	recut	recutting
redo	redoes	redid	redone	redoing
redraw	redraws	redrew	redrawn	redrawing

Infinitive	3rd Person Singular Present	Past Tense	Past Participle	Present Participle
refreeze	refreezes	refroze	refrozen	refreezing
regrow	regrows	regrew	regrown	regrowing
relight	relights	relit	relit	relighting
remake	remakes	remade	remade	remaking
rend	rends	rent	rent	rending
repay	repays	repaid	repaid	repaying
reread	rereads	reread	reread	rereading
rerun	reruns	reran	rerun	rerunning
resell	resells	resold	resold	reselling
reset	resets	reset	reset	resetting
reshoot	reshoots	reshot	reshot	reshooting
respell	respells	respelled, respelt	respelled, respelt	respelling
restring	restrings	restrung	restrung	restringing
retake	retakes	retook	retaken	retaking
retell	retells	retold	retold	retelling
rethink	rethinks	rethought	rethought	rethinking
rewind	rewinds	rewound	rewound	rewinding
rewrite	rewrites	rewrote	rewritten	rewriting
rid	rids	rid	rid	ridding
ride	rides	rode	ridden	riding

Infinitive	3rd Person Singular Present	Past Tense	Past Participle	Present Participle
ring (*sound*)	rings	rang	rung	ringing
ring (*surround*)	rings	ringed	ringed	ringing
rise	rises	rose	risen	rising
RSVP	RSVP's	RSVP'd	RSVP'd	RSVP'ing
rumba	rumbas	rumbaed, rumba'd	rumbaed, rumba'd	rumbaing
run	runs	ran	run	running
samba	sambas	sambaed, samba'd	sambaed, samba'd	sambaing
saw	saws	sawed	sawn, sawed	sawing
say	says	said	said	saying
see	sees	saw	seen	seeing
seek	seeks	sought	sought	seeking
sell	sells	sold	sold	selling
send	sends	sent	sent	sending
set	sets	set	set	setting
sew	sews	sewed	sewn, sewed	sewing
shake	shakes	shook	shaken	shaking
shave	shaves	shaved	shaved, shaven	shaving
shear	shears	sheared	shorn, sheared	shearing
shed	sheds	shed	shed	shedding
shellac	shellacs	shellacked	shellacked	shellacking

Infinitive	3rd Person Singular Present	Past Tense	Past Participle	Present Participle
shine (glow)	shines	shone	shone	shining
shine (polish shoes)	shines	shined	shined	shining
shoe	shoes	shod, shoed	shod, shoed	shoeing
shoot	shoots	shot	shot	shooting
show	shows	showed	shown	showing
shrink	shrinks	shrank	shrunk	shrinking
shut	shuts	shut	shut	shutting
simulcast	simulcasts	simulcast	simulcast	simulcasting
sing	sings	sang	sung	singing
sink	sinks	sank	sunk	sinking
sit	sits	sat	sat	sitting
slay	slays	slew	slain	slaying
sleep	sleeps	slept	slept	sleeping
slide	slides	slid	slid	sliding
sling	slings	slung	slung	slinging
slink	slinks	slunk	slunk	slinking
slit	slits	slit	slit	slitting
smite	smites	smote	smitten	smiting
sneak	sneaks	snuck, sneaked	snuck, sneaked	sneaking
sow	sows	sowed	sown, sowed	sowing

Infinitive	3rd Person Singular Present	Past Tense	Past Participle	Present Participle
speak	speaks	spoke	spoken	speaking
speed	speeds	sped, speeded	sped, speeded	speeding
spell (write)	spells	spelled, spelt	spelled, spelt	spelling
spell (relieve)	spells	spelled	spelled	spelling
spellbind	spellbinds	spellbound	spellbound	spellbinding
spend	spends	spent	spent	spending
spill	spills	spilled, split	spilled, split	spilling
spin	spins	spun	spun	spinning
spit (expectorate)	spits	spat, spit	spat, spit	spitting
split	splits	split	split	splitting
spotlight	spotlights	spotlighted, spotlit	spotlighted, spotlit	spotlighting
spread	spreads	spread	spread	spreading
spring	springs	sprang, sprung	sprung	springing
stand	stands	stood	stood	standing
stave	staves	stove, staved	stove, staved	staving
steal	steals	stole	stolen	stealing
stick	sticks	stuck	stuck	sticking
sting	stings	stung	stung	stinging
stink	stinks	stank, stunk	stunk	stinking
strew	strews	strewed	strewn, strewed	strewing

Infinitive	3rd Person Singular Present	Past Tense	Past Participle	Present Participle
stride	strides	strode	stridden	striding
strike	strikes	struck	struck	striking
string	strings	strung	strung	stringing
strive	strives	strove, strived	striven	striving
sublet	sublets	sublet	sublet	subletting
swear	swears	swore	sworn	swearing
sweat	sweats	sweated, sweat	sweated, sweat	sweating
sweep	sweeps	swept	swept	sweeping
swell	swells	swelled	swollen, swelled	swelling
swim	swims	swam	swum	swimming
swing	swings	swung	swung	swinging
TA	TA's	TA'd	TA'd	TA'ing
tailspin	tailspins	tailspun	tailspun	tailspinning
take	takes	took	taken	taking
tarmac	tarmacs	tarmacked	tarmacked	tarmacking
teach	teaches	taught	taught	teaching
tear (*rip*)	tears	tore	torn	tearing
telecast	telecasts	telecast	telecast	telecasting
tell	tells	told	told	telling
think	thinks	thought	thought	thinking

Infinitive	3rd Person Singular Present	Past Tense	Past Participle	Present Participle
thrive	thrives	thrived, throve	thrived	thriving
throw	throws	threw	thrown	throwing
thrust	thrusts	thrust	thrust	thrusting
TKO	TKO's	TKO'd	TKO'd	TKO'ing
traffic	traffics	trafficked	trafficked	trafficking
tread	treads	trod	trodden, trod	treading
troubleshoot	troubleshoots	troubleshot	troubleshot	troubleshooting
typecast	typecasts	typecast	typecast	typecasting
typeset	typesets	typeset	typeset	typesetting
unbend	unbends	unbent	unbent	unbending
underbid	underbids	underbid	underbid	underbidding
undercut	undercuts	undercut	undercut	undercutting
undergo	undergoes	underwent	undergone	undergoing
underlay	underlays	underlaid	underlaid	underlaying
underlie	underlies	underlay	underlain	underlying
underpay	underpays	underpaid	underpaid	underpaying
undersell	undersells	undersold	undersold	underselling
understand	understands	understood	understood	understanding
undertake	undertakes	undertook	undertaken	undertaking
underwrite	underwrites	underwrote	underwritten	underwriting

Infinitive	3rd Person Singular Present	Past Tense	Past Participle	Present Participle
undo	undoes	undid	undone	undoing
unfreeze	unfreezes	unfroze	unfrozen	unfreezing
unlearn	unlearns	unlearned, unlearnt	unlearned, unlearnt	unlearning
unmake	unmakes	unmade	unmade	unmaking
unstick	unsticks	unstuck	unstuck	unsticking
unstring	unstrings	unstrung	unstrung	unstringing
unwind	unwinds	unwound	unwound	unwinding
uphold	upholds	upheld	upheld	upholding
uppercut	uppercuts	uppercut	uppercut	uppercutting
upset	upsets	upset	upset	upsetting
wake	wakes	woke, waked	woken, waked	waking
waylay	waylays	waylaid	waylaid	waylaying
wear	wears	wore	worn	wearing
weave (make fabric)	weaves	wove	woven, wove	weaving
weave (zigzag)	weaves	weaved, wove	weaved, woven	weaving
wed	weds	wedded, wed	wedded, wed	wedding
weep	weeps	wept	wept	weeping
wet	wets	wet, wetted	wet, wetted	wetting
whipsaw	whipsaws	whipsawed	whipsawed, whipsawn	whipsawing
win	wins	won	won	winning

Infinitive	3rd Person Singular Present	Past Tense	Past Participle	Present Participle
wind (*twist*)	winds	wound	wound	winding
withdraw	withdraws	withdrew	withdrawn	withdrawing
withhold	withholds	withheld	withheld	withholding
withstand	withstands	withstood	withstood	withstanding
wring	wrings	wrung	wrung	wringing
write	writes	wrote	written	writing

Appendix 3: The Language of Literary Criticism

Figurative language

Imagery is language that produces pictures in the mind. The term can be used to discuss the various stylistic devices listed below, especially **figures of speech** (ways of using language to convey or suggest a meaning beyond the literal meaning of the words).

Metaphor is the imaginative use of a word or phrase to describe something else, to show that the two have the same qualities:

All the world's a stage
And all the men and women merely players
            (William Shakespeare, *As You Like It*)

In **simile** the comparison between the two things is made explicit by the use of the words *as* or *like*:

I wandered lonely as a cloud
            (William Wordsworth, *Daffodils*)

Like as the waves make towards the pebbled shore,
So do our minutes hasten to their end.
            (Shakespeare, Sonnet 60)

Metonymy is the fact of referring to something by the name of something else closely connected with it, used especially as a form of shorthand for something familiar or obvious, as in *I've been reading Shakespeare* instead of *I've been reading the plays of Shakespeare.*

Allegory is a style of writing in which each character or event is a symbol representing a particular quality. In John Bunyan's *Pilgrim's Progress,* Christian escapes from the City of Destruction, travels though the Slough of Despond, visits Vanity Fair and finally arrives at the

Celestial City. He meets characters such as the Giant Despair and Mr. Worldly Wiseman and is accompanied by Faithful and Hopeful.

Personification is the act of representing objects or qualities as human beings:

> *Love bade me welcome: yet my soul drew back,*
> *Guilty of dust and sin.*
>> (George Herbert, *Love*)

Pathetic fallacy is the effect produced when animals and things are shown as having human feelings. For example, in John Milton's poem, *Lycidas*, the flowers are shown as weeping for the dead shepherd, Lycidas.

Patterns of sound

Alliteration is the use of the same letter or sound at the beginning of words that are close together. It was used systematically in Old English poetry but in modern English poetry is generally used only for a particular effect:

> *On the bald street breaks the blank day.*
>> (Alfred, Lord Tennyson, *In Memoriam*)

Assonance is the effect created when two syllables in words that are close together have the same vowel sound but different consonants, or the same consonants but different vowels:

> *It seemed that out of the battle I escaped*
> *Down some profound dull tunnel long since scooped...*
>> (Wilfred Owen, *Strange Meeting*)

Onomatopoeia is the effect produced when the words used contain similar sounds to the noises they describe:

> *murmuring of innumerable bees*
>> (Tennyson, *The Princess*)

Other stylistic effects

Irony is the use of words that say the opposite of what you really mean, often in order to make a critical comment.

Hyperbole is the use of exaggeration:
> *An hundred years should go to praise*
> *Thine eyes and on thy forehead gaze*
>> (Andrew Marvell, *To His Coy Mistress*)

An **oxymoron** is a phrase that combines two words that seem to be the opposite of each other:
> *Parting is such sweet sorrow*
>> (Shakespeare, *Romeo and Juliet*)

A **paradox** is a statement that contains two opposite ideas or seems to be impossible:
> *The Child is father of the Man.*
>> (Wordsworth, "My heart leaps up...")

Poetry

Lyric poetry is usually fairly short and expresses thoughts and feelings. Examples are Wordsworth's *Daffodils* and Dylan Thomas's *Fern Hill*.

Epic poetry can be much longer and deals with the actions of great men and women or the history of nations. Examples are Homer's *Iliad* and Virgil's *Aeneid*.

Narrative poetry tells a story, like Chaucer's *Canterbury Tales,* or Coleridge's *Rime of the Ancient Mariner.*

Dramatic poetry takes the form of a play, and includes the plays of Shakespeare (which also contain scenes in **prose**).

A **ballad** is a traditional type of narrative poem with short **verses** or **stanzas** and a simple **rhyme scheme** (pattern of rhymes).

An **elegy** is a type of lyric poem that expresses sadness for someone who has died. Thomas Gray's *Elegy Written in a Country Churchyard* mourns all who lived and died quietly and never had a chance to be great.

An **ode** is a lyric poem that addresses a person or thing or celebrates an event. John Keats wrote five great odes, including *Ode to a Nightingale, Ode on a Grecian Urn,* and *To Autumn.*

Metre is the rhythm of poetry determined by the arrangement of stressed and unstressed, or long and short, syllables in each line of the poem.

Prosody is the theory and study of metre.

Iambic pentameter is the most common metre in English poetry. Each line consists of five **feet** (pentameter), each containing an unstressed syllable followed by a stressed syllable (iambic):

> The curfew tolls the knell of parting day
>   (Gray's *Elegy*)

Most lines of iambic pentameter, however, are not absolutely regular in their pattern of stresses:

> Shall I compare thee to a summer's day?
>   (Shakespeare, *Romeo and Juliet*)

A **sonnet** is a poem of 14 lines, in English written in iambic pentameter, and with a fixed pattern of rhyme, often ending with a rhyming couplet.

Blank verse is poetry written in iambic pentameters that do not rhyme. A lot of Shakespeare's dramatic verse is in blank verse, as is Milton's epic *Paradise Lost.*

Free verse is poetry without a regular metre or rhyme scheme. Much contemporary poetry is written in free verse, for example T.S. Eliot's *The Waste Land.*

Drama

The different **genres** of drama include **comedy, tragedy,** and **farce.**

Catharsis is the process of releasing and providing release from strong emotions such as pity and fear by watching the same emotions being played out on stage.

A **deus ex machina** is an unexpected power or situation that suddenly appears to resolve a situation that seems hopeless. It is often used to talk about a character in a play or story who only appears at the end.

Dramatic irony is when a character's words carry an extra meaning, especially because of what is going to happen that the character does not know about. For example, King Duncan in Shakespeare's *Macbeth* is pleased to accept Macbeth's hospitality, not knowing that Macbeth is going to murder him that night.

Hubris is too much pride or self-confidence, especially when shown by a tragic hero or heroine who tries to defy the gods or fate.

Nemesis is what happens when the hero or heroine's past mistakes or sins finally cause his or her downfall or death.

A **soliloquy** is a speech in a play for one character who is alone on the stage and speaks his or her thoughts aloud. The most famous soliloquy in English drama is Hamlet's beginning "To be or not to be..."

Narrative

A **novel** is a **narrative** (a story) long enough to fill a complete book. The story may be told by a **first-person narrator,** who is a character in the story and relates what happens to himself or herself, or there may be an **omniscient narrator** who relates what happens to all of the characters in the third person.

A **short story** is a story that is short enough to read from beginning to end without stopping.

The **denouement** is the end of a book or play in which everything is explained or settled. It is often used to talk about mystery or detective stories.

Stream of consciousness is a style of writing used in novels that shows the continuous flow of a character's thoughts and feelings without using the usual methods of description or conversation. It was used particularly in the twentieth century by writers such as James Joyce and Virginia Woolf.

PRAISE FOR THE
CANADIAN OXFORD DICTIONARY

"...a unique reference book for all Canadians; an essential tool for anyone writing for Canadian readers; and a book I know I will consult endlessly."

Robert MacNeil, *Time Magazine*

"It is a treat to find the way we speak validated in a thick, stylish, authoritative volume which can take its place on the bookshelf with other great dictionaries... On the evidence of a week's serious browsing, the Canadian Oxford earns an A."

Winnipeg Free Press

"We can all write and speak a bit more confidently with the arrival of the *Canadian Oxford Dictionary*."

The Globe and Mail

"The *Canadian Oxford Dictionary*... has set new standards in Canadian lexicography while unexpectedly shooting to the top of bestseller lists."

Toronto Star

"Canadian libraries will want to update their reference collections with the latest edition, which is also a worthy addition to any Canadian home reference collection."

Booklist

Official Dictionary of
The Canadian Press and *The Globe and Mail*

Over 200,000 copies sold

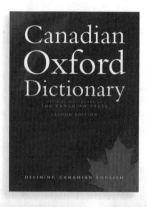
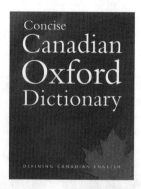
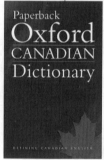
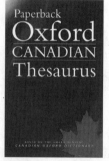
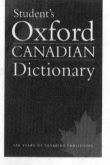

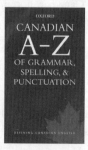